RICHMOND

W9-BVK-221

IT'S
ALL
EASY

ALSO BY GWYNETH PALTROW

My Father's Daughter

It's All Good

IT'S ALL EASY

DELICIOUS WEEKDAY RECIPES
for the SUPER-BUSY
HOME COOK

GWYNETH PALTROW

With THEA BAUMANN

Photographs by DITTE ISAGER

goop
press

GRAND CENTRAL
Life & Style
NEW YORK • BOSTON

05/16

ATLANTIC CITY FREE PUBLIC LIBRARY

Copyright © 2016 by Gwyneth Paltrow

Photographs copyright © 2016 by Ditte Isager

All rights reserved. In accordance with the U.S. Copyright Act of 1976, the scanning, uploading, and electronic sharing of any part of this book without the permission of the publisher constitute unlawful piracy and theft of the author's intellectual property. If you would like to use material from the book (other than for review purposes), prior written permission must be obtained by contacting the publisher at permissions@hbgusa.com. Thank you for your support of the author's rights.

Grand Central Life & Style
Hachette Book Group
1290 Avenue of the Americas
New York, NY 10104

www.GrandCentralLifeandStyle.com

Printed in the United States of America

Q-MA

First Edition: April 2016

10 9 8 7 6 5 4 3 2 1

Grand Central Life & Style is an imprint of Grand Central Publishing. The Grand Central Life & Style name and logo are trademarks of Hachette Book Group, Inc.

The Hachette Speakers Bureau provides a wide range of authors for speaking events. To find out more, go to www.HachetteSpeakersBureau.com or call (866) 376-6591.

The publisher is not responsible for websites (or their content) that are not owned by the publisher.

Library of Congress Cataloging-in-Publication Data

Names: Paltrow, Gwyneth, 1972- author. | Baumann, Thea, author.
Title: It's all easy : delicious weekday recipes for the super-busy home cook / Gwyneth Paltrow with Thea Baumann ; photographs by Ditte Isager.
Description: First edition. | Boston : Life & Style, [2016] | Includes index.
Identifiers: LCCN 2015044440 | ISBN 978-1-4555-8421-5 (hardcover) | ISBN 978-1-4555-8422-2 (ebook)
Subjects: LCSH: Quick and easy cooking. | LCGFT: Cookbooks.
Classification: LCC TX833.5 .P35 2016 | DDC 641.5/12-dc23 LC record available at http://lccn.loc.gov/2015044440

ISBN 978-1-4555-4193-5 (hardcover, signed edition)
ISBN 978-1-4555-4192-8 (hardcover, Barnes & Noble signed edition)

BOOK AND JACKET DESIGN BY SHUBHANI SARKAR
sarkardesignstudio.com

33352004386740

For Whistler and Eliel. For Mimi and Mac and Ben. For Elle, Lou Lou, Elijah, and Isaiah. For Sam and Margo. For William, Fiona, Peter, Georgia, Penelope, and Simon. For Bailey, Beckett, Reilly, and Miller; for Ella and Silvan. And for Sascha, Julian, and Shepard. And Stella. And Sophia. And Willow and Izzy. And Izzy and Brody. For Loftin and Emmett. For Ellie, Frances, and Connor. For Deven, Fiene, Ava, Emily, Marine, Dylan, Freddy, Maverick, Andrew, Ben, and Boone. For Rudi and Theo. For Matthew and John Owen; for Ford and Logan. For Kate and Sparrow; for Olive, and Frankie. For Blue. For Emma and Roman. For Bee, and for Mafalda, Olimpia, and Tassilo. For Brewer and Peyton. For Lucy, George, and Oggie; and for Theo, Olivia, and Sabrina. For Elliot and Harper, James and Peter. For Grace and Liam. And for the ones who are yet a twinkle in their parents' eye or a bun in the oven.

Apple and Moses, this book is for you.

CONTENTS

INTRODUCTION

KEEPING IT EASY

By Gwyneth Paltrow

What does "easy" mean in the context of being in the kitchen and preparing food?

How does one do it—create ease among the pots, appliances, fresh food, and pantry items—when we so often arrive in that particular heart of the house brimming with worries about time and preparedness, execution and outcome? "Easy" implies a lack of complications or obstacles. The kitchen seems laden with both. But let me back up.

When I sat down to start this book, I had been polling my friends and colleagues on what sort of cookbook they were looking for. These friends all seemed to have a common culinary yearning: They wanted a collection of recipes that they could prepare easily. They wanted to find themselves in the kitchen at the end of their overextended day and be able to prepare something delicious and quick.

Their lives are packed with responsibility and work and children. And yet, they were not willing to give up on the moment—the small and beautiful moment of preparing food with some care, by one's own hand, and sitting down to eat it with the people they love. Essentially, they yearned for the moment that is the antidote to all their busyness. A simple reset of the compass toward wholeness and quality at the end of the day, before the next morning comes, bringing with it the dizziness of being pulled in so many directions, a splitting of priorities.

How to integrate "busy" (anxiety, fullness of schedule, responsibility) with quality of inner life seems to be the issue on the table (so to speak). It's almost as if the more we pile on our plates, the deeper we long for the simpler aspects of life, which makes perfect sense. But how can we achieve this balance?

Everywhere I go, everyone seems to be inundated with obligation. Everyone is under an intense amount of pressure to do multiple things simultaneously, and to be doing them to an impossibly high standard. It seems to be a facet of life for our generation: hyper-responsibility. I'm not quite sure why we have done this to ourselves or how/why this drive was imparted to us, but we seem to be living lives where our self-imposed standards leave little time for daydreams and meanderings. We yearn for that lost aspect of life, before smartphones hijacked picnics and walks on the beach. Before media, in all its new forms, made you so aware of what everyone else was doing that the magic of solitude gave rise to FOMO*.

My friends said that they want to make good food quickly and easily, but what are they really saying? What is the feeling they are seeking? A road map, perhaps, for a way back to something. That warm wash of simplicity. It takes effort to carve out those moments, and increasingly we need a framework from which we can hang them. Good food at a table can provide that framework.

The food doesn't need to be complicated to be good. You don't need to work for days to create that feeling of wholeness. There has been many a night when I have stood in front of the open pantry, totally at a loss for what to throw together, and settled on pasta with butter and cheese, or a can of organic tomato soup and a grilled cheese, or frozen Amy's pizza bites.

---

* Fear of missing out.

Meaning, I've done the best I can on that particular day, and gone really easy on myself…with a large glass of wine on the side and no guilt.

This book is meant to be a road map: a self-help book for the chronically busy cook. With the extraordinary support of my cohort, Thea Baumann, I bring you *It's All Easy*, and it aims to make your time in the kitchen just that. Although the food in this book tends to be on the healthier side (see the gluten-free, dairy-free dessert section), we have also included recipes with more standard ingredients (some cheese, some regular flour) because, well, it's just easier. And because we never sacrifice deliciousness, some of these recipes might have an extra step or a special ingredient that might not seem super easy, but trust us, it's worth it.

My friend Crystal Lourd ends her emails with a phrase I love. When we are trying to decide who is bringing what to the fourth-grade-class faculty appreciation potluck, trying to coordinate a last-minute playdate for our boys, or aiming to sneak in a glass of wine and a chat, she signs off with "Keep easy." It's a phrase that instantly gives comfort and takes the pressure off. That's the idea here: Approach the kitchen with an air of easiness. Because even if life isn't all easy—far from it—sitting down and enjoying a good meal with people you really like can be. It should be.

MAKING SURE IT WORKS

By Thea Baumann

When Gwyneth first asked if I'd be interested in coauthoring this cookbook, my jaw nearly hit the floor. Anyone who knows me well knows that this opportunity was literally a dream come true. It was, however, also kind of terrifying. While I'd written recipes for private clients in the past, and was busily writing recipes as the food editor for GOOP, I'd never worked on a cookbook and was frankly a little daunted by the idea.

Gwyneth, or GP as we call her, the consummate pro, quickly set my mind at ease. She explained, in her characteristically nonchalant manner, that, in simple terms, writing a cookbook is a pretty straightforward undertaking: we cook, we write down what we did, we test, we tweak, and we retest. Since the theme of the book is easy weekday meals, I started writing down recipes I made for dinner that she and the kids loved, and she did the same. We set aside time during the day to cook together, enlisting guitar teachers, houseguests, and kids over for slumber parties as taste-testers, and compared notes about recipe ideas and inspiration. We then roped in willing friends, family (I think between them, my sisters made every single recipe in this book), and pretty much the entire GOOP team to test and give feedback, and, slowly but surely, the book began to take form.

With a name like *It's All Easy*, you might expect this to be full of recipes with five ingredients that can be made in under twenty minutes. It's not. What it is, however, is a book thoughtfully developed by two busy women who understand the importance of a good, simple meal. These recipes are easy, healthy, and approachable for cooks with any lifestyle and any skill level. We made them as quick and simple as possible without ever compromising on taste or quality, because while efficiency is key, we still want everything we eat and make for our families to be delicious and good for us. Otherwise, what's the point?

As a minor (read: major) cookbook addict, I can spend hours poring over beautiful pages full of obscure ingredients and complicated techniques. But the books that I actually reach for when I want to cook, the ones with worn bindings and food spills on the pages, are the simple ones. They're the books full of great flavors and unpretentious ingredients; the ones with recipes that I can shop for and get on the table without giving up an entire day. Our aim here was to make a book like that—a book full of recipes that are beautiful and sometimes unexpected, while also comforting, satisfying, and realistic for anyone and everyone to make. If we've done our job, which I sincerely hope we have, this book will live in your kitchen, its pages stained with anchovy oil and stuck together with egg white. I hope you have as much fun cooking from it as we had making it.

SOME INGREDIENTS AND TOOLS WE USE IN THIS BOOK

Part of the secret to making really good, easy food is making sure your kitchen is stocked with ingredients, some of which are not run-of-the-mill. (Have you ever truly known the umami-packed complexity of fish sauce, or what gochujang paste can do to an otherwise average sauce?) Yeah, it takes time to procure all these bottles, pastes, and seasonings, but one trip to the Asian grocery store (in person or online) and a big stock-up at Whole Foods or other specialty food shop will enable you to make quick, easy, and authentic-tasting dishes for months.

Please note: We have labelled many recipes "Gluten-free" because they don't contain wheat, barley, or rye, but be sure to check product labels—particularly of condiments—for gluten (wheat or barley derivatives) when purchasing.

OILS

Coconut oil

Hazelnut oil

Olive oil
(We always use organic extra-virgin.)

Peanut oil

Safflower oil

Toasted sesame oil

White truffle oil

VINEGARS

Apple cider vinegar

Balsamic vinegar

Champagne vinegar

Red wine vinegar

Rice wine vinegar

CONDIMENTS AND SAUCES

Dashi
(This seasoning liquid is the base for most of our ramens. Made from soy and bonito, it's full of umami flavor.)

Dijon mustard

Fish sauce

Gochujang paste
(a spicy Korean red pepper paste great for sauces and marinades)

Grainy mustard

Ketchup

Kimchi

Mirin

Miso (white and red)

Ponzu

Sambal oelek
(a chili paste—look for it at Asian supermarkets or online)

Sriracha

Tahini

Tamari (a naturally gluten-free soy sauce)

Vegenaise

Worcestershire sauce

CANNED GOODS

Anchovies

Beans
(including cannellini, chickpeas, and black beans)

Canned tomatoes

Capers

Chicken stock

Chipotles in adobo

Olives (niçoise and kalamata)

Sun-dried tomatoes
(oil packed)

Tomato paste

Tuna (oil-packed)

RICES, PASTAS, FLOURS, AND OTHER PANTRY ITEMS

Bonito flakes
(dried, fermented, smoked, and thinly shaved skipjack tuna…lends incredible flavor to ramen)

Bread crumbs
(panko and regular)

Brown rice

Buckwheat groats

Chia seeds

Chickpea flour

Coconut flour

Dried chipotle chili peppers

Dried pasta
(spaghetti, bucatini, rigatoni, orecchiette; we like De Cecco best)

Dried shiitakes

Farro

Fresh egg noodles
(for ramen)
Gluten-free oats
(old-fashioned and
quick-cooking)
Gluten-free pancake mix
Hemp seeds
Instant polenta
Nori sheets
Quinoa
Raw nuts
Rice noodles
White rice

GO-TO PRODUCE
Avocados
Fresh herbs
Ginger
Jalapeños
Lemons
Limes
Onions
Scallions
Shallots

IN THE FREEZER
Bacon or pancetta
Coconut ice cream
Fruits
Peas

FOR DESSERTS
Almond butter
Almond meal/flour
Brown rice syrup
Coconut milk
Coconut sugar
Date syrup
Honey, preferably manuka
Kuzu root
(a vegan, natural,
unprocessed thickening

agent used in place of
gelatin)
Liquid stevia
Maple syrup
Raw cacao or unsweetened
cocoa powder
Unsweetened shredded
coconut

THE SPICE SHELF
Aleppo pepper
Cardamom pods
Cayenne pepper
Chili flakes
Chili powder
Chipotle chili powder
Cinnamon sticks
Coriander
Cumin
Curry powder
Garam masala
Harissa powder
Madras curry powder
Mexican oregano
Mustard powder
Nutmeg
Saffron
Sesame seeds
Sumac
Tandoori spice
(An Indian spice mix usually
made with paprika, ground
cumin, ground coriander,
ground cinnamon, and/or
cardamom and ground
ginger. Whole Foods sells
a good one.)
Vanilla extract
Wasabi powder
Whole cloves
Za'atar
(a Middle Eastern spice

blend usually made with
dried thyme, oregano,
toasted sesame seeds,
sumac, and salt)

ALCOHOL FOR COOKING
Sake
Sherry
White wine

TOOLS
Bamboo matcha whisk
(the traditional tool for
making matcha tea)
Food processor
Immersion blender
Microplane rasp grater
(an affordable and
indispensable tool—use it
to grate lemon zest
and "finely mince" ginger
and garlic)
Spiralizer
(We're obsessed with this
tool and use it to make
noodles out of all kinds of
veggies, especially zucchini.)
Vitamix blender
(Expensive, but worth it.
We use this to blend
all our soups and to make
cashew cream, among
other things.)

IT'S
ALL
EASY

FIRST THING

Breakfast is widely considered the most important meal of the day, especially for kids. It provides essential fuel for our brains and bodies and also gets our metabolism working. As a busy mom trying to make healthy choices, though, it's often the meal I struggle with the most. Sure, a frozen waffle, toasted bagel, or quick bowl of cereal are all breakfast standbys for a reason, but these carb- and sugar-loaded options don't offer the sustained energy we need to function at our best. The recipes in this chapter, like Ginger Chia Pudding (page 15), Migas (page 10), and Pitaya Bowl (page 17), are almost as quick to prepare and way better for you. These easy breakfast recipes help my kids concentrate at school and keep me from passing out in my morning cardio class.

AÇAI BOWL

Vegan, Gluten-free, Under 30 minutes
SERVES 1

These little antioxidant-packed smoothie bowls are really quick to put together and totally customizable—you can top them with whatever fruits, grains, or nuts you like.

1 teaspoon coconut oil

2 tablespoons large unsweetened coconut flakes

1 (3.5-ounce) pack frozen açai berries

1 banana

2 tablespoons rice milk

1 Medjool date, pitted

1 tablespoon almond butter

1 tablespoon chia seeds

2 tablespoons gluten-free granola, homemade (page 252) or store-bought

2 tablespoons dried goji berries

Other toppings of your choice

In a sauté pan, melt the coconut oil over medium-low heat. Add the coconut flakes and toast for 2 to 3 minutes, until lightly browned. Transfer to a plate and set aside.

Break up the açai pack into large chunks and drop them into a high-powered blender. Add the banana, rice milk, date, and almond butter; blend until smooth.

Pour the mixture into a bowl and garnish with the chia seeds, granola, goji berries, toasted coconut flakes, and any other toppings you like.

BLUEBERRY GRANOLA PARFAIT

Vegetarian, Gluten-free, Under 30 minutes

SERVES 1

While a granola parfait doesn't really require a recipe, we wanted to include it simply because it makes such a killer breakfast. I could eat this every morning. Or afternoon. Or evening, for that matter. Play around with different combinations of yogurt and fruit, and sub in your favorite store-bought granola if you don't have time to make your own.

⅓ **cup yogurt**

4 teaspoons honey

¼ **cup fresh blueberries**

¼ **cup gluten-free granola, homemade (page 252) or store-bought**

In a small mason jar, layer half the yogurt, half the honey, half the blueberries, and half the granola. Repeat.

Eat right away or keep in the fridge for up to 24 hours.

BREAKFAST CREPES

Vegetarian, Under 30 minutes
MAKES 8 CREPES

While crepes sound too fancy to be fast food, they actually are! Enlist your kids to help make these and dress them up with whatever toppings you like. We love the simple lemon and powdered sugar combo, but jam and ricotta or Nutella and banana (Moses's favorite) are also solid choices.

1 cup all-purpose flour

1¼ cups whole milk

2 large eggs

2 tablespoons granulated sugar

A large pinch of kosher salt

4 tablespoons (½ stick) unsalted butter

Fresh lemon juice, for serving

Powdered sugar, for serving

In a medium bowl with a spout, whisk together the flour, milk, eggs, granulated sugar, and salt. In an 8-inch nonstick sauté pan, melt ½ tablespoon of the butter over medium-high heat. Pour in one-eighth of the batter (about ⅛ cup) and tilt the pan to distribute the batter evenly. Cook for 1 to 2 minutes, flip the crepe, and cook for 1 minute on the second side. Transfer to a plate and top with a bit of lemon juice and a sprinkle of powdered sugar (or other toppings of your choice). Repeat with the remaining batter, using ½ tablespoon of the butter to cook each crepe and adjusting the heat as necessary to make sure the crepes get nice and brown but don't burn.

ALMOND ORANGE OVERNIGHT OATS

Vegetarian, Gluten-free, Under 30 minutes
SERVES 1

These make such a great breakfast on the go; whip them up the night before and they'll be perfectly cold and creamy in the morning.

1 tablespoon slivered almonds

1 tablespoon unsweetened coconut flakes

¼ cup gluten-free quick-cooking oats

A pinch of kosher salt

2 teaspoons maple syrup

2 tablespoons Greek yogurt

⅓ cup almond or rice milk

1 teaspoon orange zest

1 tablespoon freshly squeezed orange juice

Toast the slivered almonds and coconut flakes in a small sauté pan over medium-low heat for 2 to 3 minutes, or until lightly browned.

Transfer the almonds and coconut flakes to a bowl or small mason jar and add the remaining ingredients. Stir well, cover, and refrigerate for at least 2 hours or up to 2 days.

CHOCOLATE CINNAMON OVERNIGHT OATS

Vegan, Gluten-free, Under 30 minutes
SERVES 1

Is it muesli? Is it chia pudding? We're not quite sure how to define this hybrid breakfast bowl. Assemble it before bed in just minutes and wake up to this exceptionally delicious and nutritious breakfast. Be sure to use quick-cooking oats, as traditional rolled oats won't absorb the liquid properly.

¼ cup gluten-free quick-cooking oats

⅛ teaspoon ground cinnamon

½ teaspoon raw cacao or unsweetened Dutch-processed cocoa powder

A pinch of salt

¼ teaspoon vanilla extract

⅔ cup rice or almond milk

2 soft dates, pitted and cut or torn into small pieces

1 tablespoon freshly squeezed orange juice

1 tablespoon chia seeds

Combine all the ingredients in a bowl or mason jar and mix well to make sure the chia seeds are evenly distributed. Cover and refrigerate for at least 2 hours and up to 2 days.

FRIED EGG SANDWICH

Under 30 minutes
SERVES 4

I am so obsessed with the fried egg sandwich at Huckleberry Bakery & Café in Los Angeles that I made my own one-pan version. Be sure to use a nonstick skillet and a good sturdy spatula when you make this, and don't panic if your cheese sticks to the pan—we had some messy sandwiches and some broken yolks while testing, but the end result was always super-tasty.

6 slices bacon

1 cup finely grated Gruyère cheese

4 large eggs

Salt and freshly ground
black pepper

4 thick slices country bread

¼ to ½ cup Cheat's Aioli
(page 248)

4 small handfuls of arugula

Arrange the bacon in a single layer in a large nonstick sauté pan and set over medium-high heat. Cook the bacon until it reaches the desired crispiness, then transfer to a paper towel–lined plate.

Wipe out almost all the bacon fat from the pan and make four ¼-cup piles of cheese in the pan (they will begin to crisp up and sizzle immediately). Crack one egg directly over each pile of cheese, season generously with salt and pepper, and fry until the whites are set and the yolks are still runny (cover the pan with a lid if you like your yolks a bit more cooked).

While the eggs fry, toast the bread in a toaster.

To assemble, spread each piece of toast with 1 to 2 tablespoons of the aioli, top with a small handful of arugula and 1½ pieces of the bacon, and finish with the crispy Gruyère–fried egg combo.

MIGAS

Vegetarian, Gluten-free, Under 30 minutes
SERVES 1

Crispy tortillas for breakfast? *Si, por favor.* We love topping this Tex-Mex favorite with our Tomatillo Salsa (page 257), Fresh Salsa (page 256), or Roasted Tomato Salsa (page 254) and lots of fresh avocado. Packed with protein, good fats, and deliciousness.

1 tablespoon safflower or olive oil

2 corn tortillas, cut into 8 wedges each

2 tablespoons diced white onion

2 large eggs

Salt and freshly ground black pepper

2 tablespoons crumbled queso fresco or grated mild Cheddar

2 tablespoons chopped fresh cilantro

Hot sauce, fresh salsa or store-bought organic salsa, sliced jalapeño, and avocado, for serving (optional)

In an 8-inch nonstick pan, heat the oil over medium-high heat. When the oil is hot but not smoking, add the tortilla wedges and white onion; cook for 1 to 2 minutes, or until the onion starts to soften and the tortilla wedges start to crisp.

Crack in the eggs, season with salt and pepper, and use a spatula to stir everything together. Cook, stirring, for 1 to 2 minutes, until the eggs are almost cooked through.

Stir in the queso fresco and cilantro and transfer to a plate.

Garnish with hot sauce, fresh salsa, sliced jalapeño, and/or sliced avocado, if desired.

SCRAMBLED EGGS
WITH PARMESAN AND ARUGULA

Vegetarian, Gluten-free, Under 30 minutes
SERVES 1

Scrambled eggs are the perfect fast food. And these, dressed up with chives, Parmesan, and arugula, are particularly nice. Easy enough for a weekday morning, but elegant enough for Easter brunch…that's my kind of breakfast.

3 large eggs

Salt and freshly ground black pepper

1 tablespoon unsalted butter

1 tablespoon chopped fresh chives

3 tablespoons finely grated Parmesan cheese

A small handful of arugula

In a medium bowl, lightly beat the eggs and season them generously with salt and pepper. In a small nonstick pan, melt the butter over medium-low heat. Add the eggs and stir with a spatula to keep them moving. When the eggs are almost cooked, add the chives, Parmesan, and arugula. Stir well and transfer to a plate.

GINGER CHIA PUDDING

Vegan, Gluten-free, Under 30 minutes
SERVES 1

These creamy little puddings taste like dessert but are actually great for you. Packed with protein, fiber, antioxidants, electrolytes, vitamins, and minerals, they give us more than enough energy to get through even the busiest of mornings. This pudding lasts for 2 to 3 days in the fridge, so I like to make a couple at a time.

¼ cup chia seeds

½ teaspoon very finely grated or minced fresh ginger

¾ cup coconut water

6 tablespoons canned coconut milk

2 teaspoons coconut sugar

¼ cup diced fresh peach (optional)

Combine the chia seeds, ginger, coconut water, coconut milk, and coconut sugar in a bowl or mason jar. Stir well, and let sit in the fridge for at least 10 minutes or up to 1 day.

Serve topped with diced fresh peach, if desired.

PITAYA BOWL

Vegan, Gluten-free, Under 30 minutes
SERVES 1

Pitaya bowls are made from blended pitaya, or dragon fruit, a tropical fruit with Technicolor magenta flesh. Similar to its South American superfood sister açai, pitaya is packed with immunity-boosting vitamins and minerals, and when topped with kiwi, blackberries, and strawberries, the intense color contrast makes this breakfast bowl almost too strikingly beautiful to eat. Almost. Look for the bright pink smoothie packs in the frozen fruit section next to the açai.

1 (3.5-ounce) pack frozen pitaya (dragon fruit), broken into large pieces

1 banana

¼ cup frozen mango chunks

2 tablespoons coconut water

1 kiwi, peeled and thinly sliced

A handful of blackberries

1 strawberry, sliced

2 tablespoons gluten-free granola, homemade (page 252) or store-bought

1 tablespoon maple syrup

Combine the pitaya pack, banana, mango chunks, and coconut water in a high-powered blender; blend until smooth.

Pour the mixture into a bowl and top with the kiwi, blackberries, strawberry, granola, and maple syrup.

ON THE GO

In a dream world, I'd eat every meal at a table with a cloth napkin and silver cutlery; in reality, I'm often spreading almond butter on a rice cake while rushing out the door. On days when I'm running straight from a meeting to a soccer game, I need food that packs up easily and satisfies me without feeling heavy (which means no fast food and no sad, wilted salads from a grab 'n' go fridge). This chapter has simple recipes for soups, salads, and wraps that can be made in advance and eaten just about anywhere (including on an airplane, the toughest place to find healthy food). Many can be prepped the night before, and most use leftover ingredients like roast chicken and cooked rice, so if I plan ahead, prep is quick and painless.

BIBIMBAP SALAD

Vegetarian, Gluten-free, Under 30 minutes
SERVES 4

Okay, I admit it: I'm a kimchi junkie. I love it on top of rice dishes or stirred into soups, stews, and savory pancake batter. I've even been known to eat it by the forkful straight out of the jar. Which is why I used it not only as one of the main ingredients in our Korean rice bowl, but also as a base for the sauce. It may not be traditional, but this is one bibimbap recipe that will make any kimchi fan swoon.

FOR THE SAUCE

1 thumb-sized piece fresh ginger, peeled and roughly chopped (about 1 tablespoon)

1 small garlic clove, thinly sliced

3 scallions, thinly sliced (about ⅓ cup)

1 tablespoon gochujang (Korean red pepper paste)

1 tablespoon plus 1 teaspoon toasted sesame oil

2 tablespoons rice wine vinegar

2 tablespoons tamari

2 tablespoons water

1 teaspoon maple syrup

⅓ cup kimchi

¼ cup olive oil

Salt, to taste

FOR THE BIBIMBAP

3 tablespoons toasted sesame oil

12 shiitakes, stemmed and sliced

Salt

1 cup mung bean sprouts

4 cups lightly packed baby spinach

4 cups cooked white rice, brown rice, or quinoa

4 small or 2 large carrots, peeled and grated

Four 9-minute eggs (page 244), halved

Kimchi

Furikake seasoning (page 251)

To make the sauce, blend all the ingredients in a high-powered blender until smooth.

To make the bibimbap, heat a sauté pan over medium-high heat; add a tablespoon of toasted sesame oil, the shiitakes, and a generous pinch of salt and cook for 2 to 3 minutes. Transfer the mushrooms to a bowl and set them aside. Add another tablespoon of toasted sesame oil to the pan, then add the bean sprouts and a pinch of salt and sauté until just tender. Transfer to a bowl and set them aside. Add the final tablespoon of sesame oil, the spinach, and a generous pinch of salt, and cook until the spinach is just wilted.

Divide the rice among four bowls and arrange the grated carrots, sautéed shiitakes, bean sprouts and spinach, eggs, and kimchi on top. Garnish with furikake and serve with the sauce on the side.

CHOPPED SALADS

I can't think of a better weekday meal than a protein-packed chopped salad. The flavor combinations are endless; they're filling, healthy, and actually satisfying; and they're pretty cheap and easy to put together. When I eat chopped salads at home, I mix all the ingredients in a bowl before plating, but when I pack a salad to go (which, by the way, I do pretty much every time I travel), I arrange them so that all the ingredients stay separate and pack dressing on the side. That way, the lettuce stays crisp, nothing gets soggy, and all I have to do is dress, shake, and eat whenever I'm ready. Pretty genius, right?

To follow are two of my go-to recipes: one has a vaguely Italian flavor profile with a mustard vinaigrette; the other is loosely inspired by Mexican flavors and has a kick-ass cilantro dressing. Both are absolutely delicious.

GRILLED CHICKEN CHOPPED SALAD

Gluten-free, Under 30 minutes
SERVES 1

You could use leftover cooked chicken here, too.

FOR THE SALAD

1 cup finely chopped romaine

1 red bell pepper, roasted, peeled, and diced

1 teaspoon olive oil

A pinch of kosher salt

1 tablespoon chopped fresh basil

6 cherry tomatoes, halved

1 small chicken paillard, grilled and chopped into small pieces

½ cup cooked chickpeas (or canned)

½ cup diced blanched green beans

2 to 4 anchovies (depending on your taste), roughly chopped

1 tablespoon diced red onion (optional)

FOR THE DRESSING

1 tablespoon red wine vinegar

2 teaspoons Dijon mustard

¼ cup olive oil

Salt and freshly ground black pepper

To make the salad, place the romaine in the bottom of a bowl or storage container. In a small bowl, toss the bell pepper with the oil, salt, and basil. Carefully arrange the bell pepper mixture, cherry tomatoes, grilled chicken, chickpeas, green beans, anchovies, and red onion (if using) on top of the romaine, so that each ingredient stays separate.

(Continued)

To make the vinaigrette, whisk together the vinegar, mustard, and oil and season to taste with salt and pepper. Pack the dressing on the side, and when ready to eat, dress, shake, and enjoy!

GRILLED SHRIMP CHOPPED SALAD

Gluten-free
SERVES 1

This makes extra dressing, but I've never had a problem getting through it.

FOR THE SALAD

¼ pound peeled and deveined shrimp

1 tablespoon olive oil

Salt and freshly ground black pepper

1 cup finely chopped romaine

1 tablespoon finely diced red onion

⅓ cup ½-inch-diced English cucumber

⅓ cup sliced radishes

6 cherry tomatoes, halved

⅓ cup ½-inch-diced avocado

⅓ cup Perfectly Cooked Quinoa (page 253)

FOR THE DRESSING

⅓ cup packed chopped fresh basil

⅓ cup packed chopped fresh cilantro

2 tablespoons packed chopped fresh mint

1 scallion, sliced

Juice of 2 limes

⅓ cup olive oil

1 teaspoon agave nectar

Salt and freshly ground black pepper

To make the salad, heat a grill pan over medium-high heat. Toss the shrimp with 1 tablespoon olive oil and season with salt and pepper. Grill the shrimp for 3 to 5 minutes, or until pink with nice grill marks. Set aside to cool, then chop into ½-inch pieces.

Place the chopped romaine at the bottom of a bowl or storage container. Carefully arrange the diced red onion, diced cucumber, sliced radishes, halved cherry tomatoes, diced avocado, quinoa, and chopped grilled shrimp on top of the romaine, so that each ingredient stays separate.

To make the dressing, combine the basil, cilantro, mint, scallion, lime juice, olive oil, and agave in a high-powered blender and blend until smooth; season with salt and pepper to taste.

Pack the dressing on the side, and when ready to eat, dress, shake, and enjoy!

KYE'S-STYLE WRAPS

Jeanne Cheng runs a great lunch spot in Santa Monica called Kye's, where she and her team use nori, romaine, and collard greens to make delicious and healthy wraps. Inspired by them, we developed these recipes, which happen to travel really well.

CHICKEN SALAD NORI WRAP

Gluten-free

MAKES 4 WRAPS

If you don't have cooked chicken on hand, skip it or use sliced tofu instead.

FOR THE SAUCE

3 tablespoons red miso paste

2 tablespoons hot water

1 tablespoon neutral oil, such as safflower

4 small or 2 large garlic cloves, very finely grated

4 teaspoons brown rice vinegar

1 tablespoon toasted sesame oil

¼ cup mirin

2 tablespoons maple syrup

FOR THE WRAP

1 cup finely shredded green cabbage

1 large carrot, peeled and grated

⅓ cup thinly sliced baby bok choy (about 2)

½ cup shredded cooked chicken

¼ cup sliced scallions

3 tablespoons toasted sesame seeds

¼ cup chopped fresh cilantro

4 sheets nori

2 cups cooked white rice, slightly cooled

To make the sauce, combine the miso and hot water in a small ramekin and stir to dissolve. Meanwhile, in a small saucepan, heat the neutral oil over medium heat; add the garlic and cook for 1 to 2 minutes, or until very fragrant and just starting to brown. Add the miso, vinegar, sesame oil, mirin, and maple syrup and turn up the heat to medium-high. Let the mixture simmer and bubble away for 5 to 10 minutes, or until thick. Remove from the heat and let the sauce cool while you assemble the wraps.

To make the wraps, put the cabbage, carrot, bok choy, cooked chicken, scallions, sesame seeds, and cilantro in a bowl and toss to combine.

(Continued)

Place the nori sheets on a flat surface and put ½ cup of the rice on each one. Wet your fingers and use them to spread the rice evenly over each sheet, going all the way to the edges horizontally, but leaving a 1½-inch border on the top and bottom. Spread 1 to 2 tablespoons of the cooled sauce over the rice, then divide the cabbage mixture among the four sheets. Carefully roll up each one, wetting the edge of the nori sheet with water so it sticks to itself and wraps snugly.

VEGETARIAN COLLARD WRAPS

Vegan, Gluten-free, Under 30 minutes

MAKES 1 WRAP

We like to cut the fibrous rib off the collard green leaf, but feel free to skip that step if you don't mind a little more crunch.

1 large or 2 small collard green leaves

¼ cup Cilantro Hummus (page 248), or your favorite store-bought hummus

⅓ cup radish sprouts or other sprouts

1 large carrot, peeled and grated

8 slices English cucumber

¼ large avocado, sliced

Coarse salt and freshly ground black pepper

Lay the collard green leaf flat on a cutting board, rib side up. Run the blade of your knife parallel to the cutting board, carefully slicing off most of the bulky rib while leaving the shape of the leaf intact.

Spread the cilantro hummus in an even layer over the middle of the wrap, leaving a 1-inch border. Layer on the sprouts, carrot, cucumber, and avocado and season the avocado with salt and a few grinds of pepper. Tuck the leafy end (opposite the rib end) over the ingredients to keep them secure, then roll up the wrap tightly like a burrito, leaving the stiffer ribbed end open.

MOROCCAN CHICKEN SALAD WRAP

Under 30 minutes

MAKES 2 LARGE OR 4 MEDIUM WRAPS

The hint of warm spices combined with the freshness of chopped cilantro makes this not your average chicken salad. And if you use rotisserie chicken, it's a snap to put together. Not reserved solely for wraps, this is almost more satisfying eaten straight from the bowl.

FOR THE CHICKEN SALAD

2 cups shredded cooked chicken (about 1 chicken breast)

1 celery stalk, finely diced

2 scallions, sliced

2 tablespoons chopped fresh cilantro

½ teaspoon ground cumin

¼ teaspoon ground cinnamon

¼ teaspoon ground coriander

6 tablespoons Vegenaise, or more to taste

1 tablespoon freshly squeezed lemon juice

1 teaspoon agave nectar

Salt and freshly ground black pepper

TO ASSEMBLE

4 tortillas, chia lavash, or your favorite wrap

4 to 8 romaine leaves, or 1 small handful of arugula

To make the chicken salad, combine all the ingredients in a large bowl and stir well. Season with salt and pepper to taste.

To assemble, lay out the tortillas. Arrange the romaine on the tortilla, top with chicken salad, and wrap.

NOODLE POTS

We did a GOOP story with Jasmine and Melissa Hemsley and fell in love with their ingenious noodle pot idea: put a bunch of fresh ingredients and seasonings in a mason jar, and when you get to work (or wherever) simply top off with boiling water for an instant, healthy soup on the go. We love the flavors of tortilla soup and Thai curry, which inspired our two versions.

TORTILLA SOUP NOODLE POT

Gluten-free, Under 30 minutes
SERVES 1

2 teaspoons tomato paste

¼ teaspoon ground cumin

¼ teaspoon chili powder

1 small corn tortilla, cut into
2 × ¼-inch strips

3 tablespoons corn kernels, cut
from a fresh ear of corn

⅓ cup spiralized zucchini noodles

2 to 3 tablespoons shredded
cooked chicken

Salt

1 heaping tablespoon chopped
fresh cilantro

¼ lime

Place the tomato paste, ground cumin, chili powder, tortilla strips, and corn in the bottom of a medium mason jar. Layer in the zucchini noodles, chicken, and a generous pinch of salt, top with the cilantro and lime wedge, and store in the fridge until ready to eat.

When ready to eat, remove the lime wedge and fill the jar with boiling water. Cover and let sit for 5 minutes. Remove the lid, squeeze in the juice from the lime wedge, and stir well, making sure the tomato paste has fully dissolved before digging in.

THAI CURRY NOODLE POT

Under 30 minutes

SERVES 1

½ teaspoon Thai red curry paste

1 teaspoon coconut oil

1 tablespoon tamari

2 tablespoons coconut milk

½ teaspoon finely grated or very finely minced fresh ginger

2 tablespoons thinly sliced snow peas

1 shiitake mushroom, thinly sliced

1 tablespoon minced shallot

⅓ cup cooked soba noodles

1 tablespoon chopped fresh cilantro

1 tablespoon chopped fresh basil

¼ lime

Place the red curry paste, coconut oil, tamari, and coconut milk in the bottom of a medium mason jar. Add the ginger, snow peas, mushroom, shallot, and soba noodles, top with the cilantro, basil, and lime wedge, and store in the fridge until ready to eat.

When ready to eat, remove the lime wedge, fill the jar with boiling water, cover, and let sit for 5 minutes. Uncover, squeeze in the juice from the lime wedge, and stir well, making sure that the curry paste has fully dissolved before digging in.

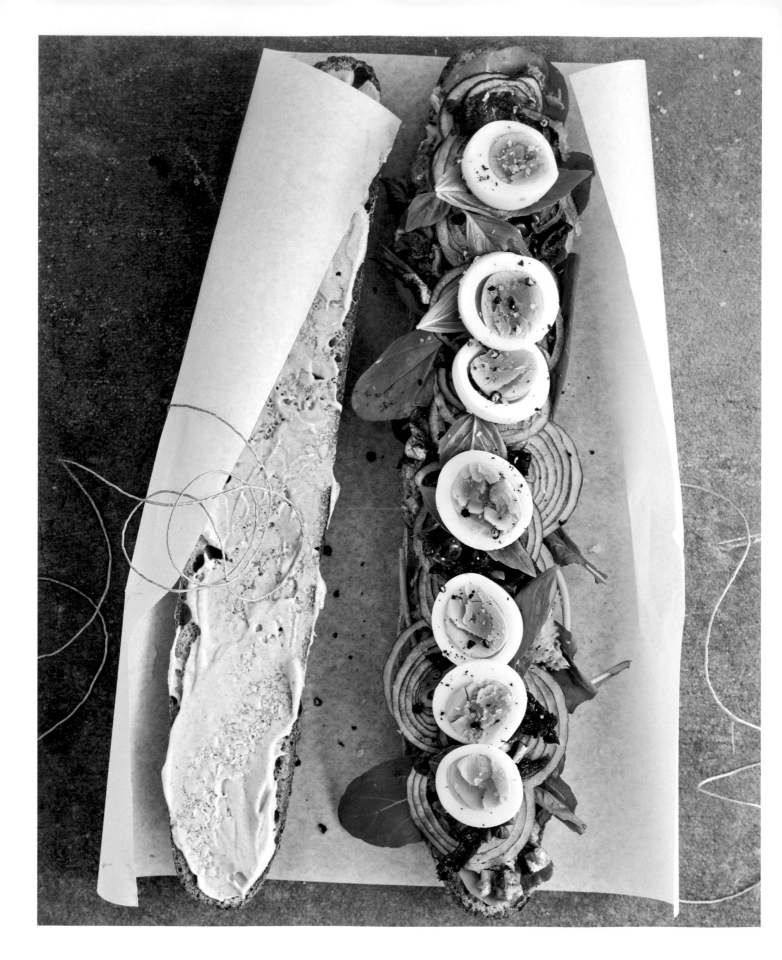

PAN BAGNAT

Under 30 minutes
SERVES 4

In simple terms, pan bagnat has all the components of a niçoise salad stuffed into a perfectly transportable sandwich form. I discovered this delight when I worked in France years ago. It is the perfect summer picnic lunch, best eaten outside on a warm day, preferably with a glass of chilled rosé in your hand. If that's out of the question, though, it's still pretty delicious eaten in the car while waiting for your kids to finish soccer practice. The quality of ingredients, particularly the tuna and baguette, really makes or breaks this sandwich, so try to find the good stuff.

1 medium baguette (about 16 inches), split lengthwise

2 tablespoons plus 2 teaspoons Dijon mustard

1 large handful of arugula

16 ounces good-quality jarred or canned tuna in olive oil

½ cup very thinly sliced red onion, or to taste

8 anchovies, roughly chopped

1 tablespoon plus 1 teaspoon capers

24 pitted niçoise (or kalamata) olives, cut in half

16 oil-packed sun-dried tomatoes

16 fresh basil leaves

Four 9-minute eggs (page 244), sliced

Salt and freshly ground black pepper

Spread each half of the baguette with a thin layer of Dijon mustard, then layer in the remaining ingredients, starting at the bottom with the arugula and finishing with the sliced eggs at the top. Season the egg with salt and pepper and press firmly to compress the sandwich. Eat right away or wrap in plastic wrap and store in the fridge for up to 24 hours. Cut into portions just before serving.

PICK-ME-UPS

While it's a different time of day for everyone, hunger pangs seem to kick in, every day, without fail. For me, it's usually around 4 p.m., when the kids are home but the workday is far from over. It's hard to know whether I'm actually hungry, stressed, or simply under-caffeinated, but whatever it is, my body craves something salty, crunchy, and usually carb-ey. It's hard to deny myself a handful of Uncle Jerry's Extra Dark Pennsylvania Dutch pretzels, even though they probably don't actually make me feel sated or more alert for very long. To contend with this tricky time of day, we came up with recipes for a couple of nutritious snacks and satisfying drinks—the perfect healthy antidotes to a blood sugar dip or a momentary lapse in focus.

AVOCADO TOAST, THREE WAYS

GP is kind of the queen of avocado toast, so we thought it would be fun to include a couple of new, dressed-up versions here. These are all great for breakfast, but I find myself eating them most often when those pesky 4 p.m. hunger pangs set in. —TB

ASIAN AVOCADO TOAST

Vegetarian, Under 30 minutes

SERVES 1

1 slice of your favorite bread

1 tablespoon Vegenaise

¼ teaspoon sriracha

¼ teaspoon toasted sesame oil

¼ to ½ avocado, depending on size, sliced

Coarse salt and freshly ground black pepper

One 7-minute egg (page 244), sliced

Furikake seasoning (page 251)

Pop your bread in the toaster and combine the Vegenaise, sriracha, and sesame oil in a small bowl. When the toast is ready, spread it with the sauce, arrange the avocado slices over the top, and season with coarse salt and pepper. Top with the egg and sprinkle with furikake.

SPRING VEGGIE AVOCADO TOAST

Vegan, Under 30 minutes
SERVES 1

Spring on a plate. We even eat this for dinner sometimes.

1 slice of your favorite bread

¼ to ½ avocado, depending on size, sliced

1 to 2 radishes, very thinly sliced

Meyer lemon or regular lemon zest

Olive oil

Coarse sea salt

Pea shoots, if available

Toast the bread. Top with the avocado, sliced radishes, lemon zest, a drizzle of olive oil, salt, and fresh pea shoots, if you can find them.

BACON AVOCADO TOAST

Under 30 minutes
SERVES 1

I thought GP was a nut when she suggested this combo, but it's crazy good. — I B

1 slice of your favorite bread

2 tablespoons almond butter

¼ to ½ avocado, depending on size, sliced

1 slice bacon, pan-fried or cooked in the oven until crispy

Toast the bread, spread it with the almond butter, arrange the avocado slices over the top, and finish with the crispy bacon.

BEET CHIPS

Vegan, Gluten-free
SERVES 4

These little snacks have all the crunchy, salty satisfaction of a potato chip and none of the guilt. Oven time depends largely on how thick your beets are sliced—so be sure to watch them carefully, and let them cool completely when they come out of the oven. They will crisp up as they sit.

1 tablespoon olive oil, plus more for the baking sheets

2 medium beets, peeled or very well scrubbed

Leaves from 1 sprig fresh rosemary, minced

Kosher salt

Cilantro Hummus (page 248)

Preheat the oven to 325°F. Grease two baking sheets lightly with olive oil.

Use a mandoline to slice the beets as thin as possible.

In a bowl, toss the beet slices with the rosemary, olive oil, and a generous pinch of salt.

Arrange the beets in an even layer on the prepared baking sheets, making sure that none of the slices overlap. If you can't fit all the slices, use another baking sheet.

Place the baking sheets in the upper and lower thirds of the oven, bake for 10 minutes, then switch their positions and bake for another 10 minutes.

Let the chips cool on the baking sheets before eating. Eat plain or with the cilantro hummus for dipping.

CHAI TEA

Vegan, Gluten-free
SERVES 4

Not your grocery store chai, this recipe is a version of one I was taught many years ago by a guy called Spiro, whom I met at Eddie Stern's yoga studio on Crosby Street in New York. I remember being blown away by the punch-you-in-the-face spice and complexity, which are tragically absent from most chai tea available here in the States. If you don't have a mortar and pestle, buy one; but in the meantime, use the bottom of a sauté pan to crush the peppercorns and other spices.

2 cinnamon sticks

10 cardamom pods

A small handful of whole cloves (about 8)

½ teaspoon whole black peppercorns

1 (2-inch) piece fresh ginger, peeled, cut into ¼-inch slices, and smashed with the back of a knife

1½ cups hot water

2 English breakfast tea bags

1 cup oat, rice, or almond milk

1 tablespoon maple syrup

Put the cinnamon sticks, cardamom pods, cloves, and peppercorns in a mortar and pound with the pestle until they are all cracked and crushed (but stop well before they become a powder).

Combine the pounded spices, fresh ginger, and hot water in a saucepan; bring to a boil, then reduce the heat and simmer gently for 15 minutes.

Add the tea bags and oat milk. Bring to a boil, then reduce the heat and simmer for 15 minutes.

Add the maple syrup and stir to dissolve. Strain the chai into mugs and enjoy.

COCONUT CAFÉ AU LAIT

Vegan, Gluten-free, Under 30 minutes
SERVES 1

When I lived in Paris, I drank a café au lait or café crème almost every morning. While I still love the original made with cow's milk, I've come to prefer this fresh coconut milk version. You can use ½ cup canned coconut milk in a pinch, but if you have a Vitamix, it's really easy and worthwhile to make your own. —TB

½ **cup freshly brewed coffee**

1 **teaspoon coconut sugar**

1 **cup Fresh Coconut Milk (page 249)**

Combine the coffee and coconut sugar in a large mug, stirring to dissolve the sugar. Meanwhile, heat the coconut milk in a small saucepan until just simmering. Add the coconut milk to the coffee, stir, and enjoy.

GINGER AND LEMON TEA

Gluten-free, Under 30 minutes
SERVES 1

This assertively spicy and citrusy tea tastes almost medicinal, in the best kind of way. I always make it when I feel a cold coming on, as the combo of honey, lemon, and ginger feels like the perfect cure for any ailment. If you use a Microplane to grate the ginger, be careful—it's the best tool for the job, but I have no skillz with a Microplane when ginger is involved…I end up grating my finger as much as the ginger in this recipe.

1 **teaspoon very finely grated fresh ginger**

1 **heaping tablespoon manuka honey**

Zest of ½ lemon, peeled with a vegetable peeler

1 **cup hot water**

Combine all the ingredients in a small saucepan. Bring the mixture to a boil, then reduce the heat and simmer for 5 minutes. Strain into a mug and enjoy.

GINGER, SESAME, AND ALMOND DRINK

Vegan, Gluten-free, Under 30 minutes
SERVES 2

When working on a GOOP story with the L.A.-based company Moon Juice, we learned the easiest-ever method for making instant almond milk: simply blend good almond butter and water together. Duh—why didn't we think of that?! Here we make a hot version with fresh ginger and a little sesame oil to add roundness—the perfect warming treat for a rainy afternoon.

1 teaspoon toasted sesame oil

1 tablespoon coconut sugar

1½ teaspoons roughly chopped fresh ginger

1 tablespoon almond butter

2 cups just-boiled water

Combine all the ingredients in a high-speed blender and blend on high until smooth. Pour into mugs and enjoy.

JESSICA'S COCONUT "LATTE"

Vegan, Gluten-free, Under 30 minutes
SERVES 1

Fellow cookbook author (and most hilarious wonderful friend) Jessica Seinfeld introduced me to this dairy-free latte.

2 tablespoons coconut oil

1 freshly brewed large espresso or small coffee

Melt the coconut oil in a small saucepan over medium heat until completely liquid. Transfer to a blender, add the hot espresso, and blitz until emulsified. Pour into a mug and enjoy.

LEMONGRASS AND MINT TISANE

Vegan, Gluten-free, Under 30 minutes
SERVES 1

Lemongrass is largely used in savory dishes, but its unique flavor adds lovely citrus notes to teas and sweet dishes as well. This lemongrass and mint infusion makes a soothing afternoon treat, but I especially love serving it at the end of a meal.

1 (4-inch) piece fresh lemongrass, tough outer layer removed

2 cups filtered water

Leaves from 6 large sprigs fresh mint, plus extra for garnish

5 drops liquid stevia (optional)

Cut the lemongrass into two 2-inch pieces and bash them with the side of a knife.

Combine the lemongrass and filtered water in a small saucepan and bring to a boil.

Add the mint leaves, turn off the heat, cover, and infuse for 10 minutes. Strain into a mug and add the stevia, if desired.

Garnish with fresh mint leaves and serve.

ROSEMARY, LEMON, AND CHILI TISANE

Gluten-free, Under 30 minutes
SERVES 1

The rosemary and chili make this tisane taste almost savory, but the brightness of lemon and sweet honey cut the spice and earthiness beautifully. We especially love this with Meyer lemon zest if you can find it.

2 large strips of lemon zest, peeled with a vegetable peeler

1 large sprig fresh rosemary

2 teaspoons honey

A small pinch of red chili flakes

1 cup filtered water

Combine all the ingredients in a small saucepan and bring to a boil. Turn off the heat, cover, and infuse for 10 minutes. Strain into a large mug and enjoy.

MATCHA TEA

Gluten-free, Under 30 minutes

SERVES 1

I try to eat healthy and detox my body as much as possible, but caffeine is one thing I hate giving up. I run on coffee in the morning, and when 4 p.m. rolls around and I start losing focus and energy, there's no pick-me-up quite like a matcha tea. This recipe is my perfect ratio of matcha, milk, and water, but the proportions can, of course, be tweaked. Warming the milk in a saucepan works just fine, but if you have a steamer, definitely use it here.

1 teaspoon matcha green tea powder

½ cup whole milk

½ cup just-boiled water

Place the matcha powder in a bowl and stir with a bamboo matcha "whisk" to break up any lumps. Meanwhile, use a steamer to steam the milk (or heat the milk in a saucepan on the stovetop); pour the milk into the bowl with the matcha and use the matcha whisk to stir well. Slowly add the hot water, whisking continuously. Transfer the tea to a mug or drink it directly from the bowl.

IN A PINCH

Cooking is one of the greatest pleasures in life, but sometimes, after a long day, it can feel like a chore. This chapter, full of recipes that require minimal effort and use a lot of pantry staples, is where I turn when all I want to do is order takeout. From Shrimp Stir-Fry (page 84) to Carbonara (page 66) to Grilled Cheese and Easy Tomato Soup (page 71), we've got you covered.

BLACK BEAN SOUP

Gluten-free, Under 30 minutes
SERVES 4

The kids absolutely love this soup, and I love it because it's so quick and simple to make. All chili powders are a little different, so we recommend starting with ¼ teaspoon of each unless you like things spicy.

3 tablespoons olive oil

1 large yellow onion, cut in half and thinly sliced

1½ teaspoons sea salt

3 large garlic cloves, sliced

12 sprigs fresh cilantro, chopped

1 teaspoon ground cumin

¼ to ½ teaspoon chili powder

¼ to ½ teaspoon chipotle chili powder

2 (15-ounce) cans black beans, drained and rinsed

3 cups low-sodium chicken stock

Grated cheese, sour cream, crispy tortilla strips, diced avocado, fresh cilantro, and fresh limes, for garnish

Heat the olive oil in a heavy-bottomed pot or Dutch oven over medium-high heat. Add the onion and salt and sauté for 5 minutes, stirring often and lowering the heat if the onion starts to brown too much. Add the garlic, cilantro, and spices, cover, and cook for 5 minutes more, checking every minute or so to make sure everything is gently sautéing and not burning.

Add the black beans and chicken stock, bring the mixture to a boil, and simmer, uncovered, for 15 minutes.

Using an immersion blender, blend the soup directly in the pot until almost completely smooth. Adjust the seasoning to taste. Serve with cheese, sour cream, tortilla strips, avocado, fresh cilantro, and fresh limes.

BREAKFAST FOR DINNER

Vegetarian, Gluten-free, Under 30 minutes
MAKES 8 SMALL PANCAKES

Breakfast for dinner always feels like a sneaky treat, and I keep a box of gluten-free pancake mix in the cupboard so I'm ready whenever the mood strikes. Eat these lemony raspberry pancakes on their own or scramble some eggs and fry up some bacon for the full diner experience—your kids (or boyfriend/wife/roommate) won't believe their luck.

1½ cups gluten-free pancake mix (we like Bob's Red Mill brand)

1 large egg

¾ cup milk (cow's, soy, almond, rice   anything you like)

1 tablespoon vegetable oil

½ cup fresh raspberries

1 teaspoon finely grated lemon zest

1 to 2 tablespoons unsalted butter, for frying the pancakes

Maple syrup, for serving

Combine the pancake mix, egg, milk, oil, raspberries, and lemon zest and mix gently, making sure not to completely crush the raspberries. In a large sauté pan, melt a bit of butter over medium heat. Use half the batter to make 4 pancakes (about ¼ cup each) and cook for 2 minutes per side. Remove to a plate and repeat with more butter and the remaining batter. Serve with maple syrup.

CARBONARA

Under 30 minutes
SERVES 4

Carbonara is the perfect lazy dinner—it's cozy, comforting, and shockingly easy to make. Not to mention the fact that everyone almost always has the ingredients on hand. Keep some cubed bacon or pancetta in the freezer so you can make this anytime, in just minutes.

Salt

4 ounces pancetta or bacon, cut into small dice

2 egg yolks (or 3, to make it extra creamy)

1 large egg

1½ cups finely grated Parmesan cheese, plus more as needed

1 teaspoon freshly ground black pepper, plus more as needed

¾ pound bucatini

Bring a large pot of heavily salted water to a boil over high heat for the pasta.

In an 8-inch sauté pan, cook the pancetta over medium heat until crispy, 5 to 7 minutes.

Combine the egg yolks, egg, Parmesan, and pepper in a large bowl.

Cook the pasta according to the package instructions until al dente. Reserve 1 cup of the hot pasta cooking water (the temperature is important because you are going to use it to cook the egg) and set aside. Next, drain the pasta, and add it to the bowl with the cheese and eggs, tossing immediately to mix everything together.

Add the pancetta and any rendered fat from the pan to the bowl, toss to coat, and add the pasta water 1 tablespoon at a time until the sauce reaches a creamy consistency (this usually takes about ¼ cup).

Adjust with extra cheese, pepper, and salt to taste.

GRILLED CHEESE AND EASY TOMATO SOUP

I haven't met a kid (or grown-up, for that matter) who doesn't love the classic combo of grilled cheese and tomato soup.

GRILLED CHEESE

Vegetarian, Under 30 minutes
SERVES 4

I like grilled cheese the English way, cooked open-faced under the broiler. Serve this with Easy Tomato Soup or your favorite canned version (shhh—we won't tell anyone).

4 slices of the bread of your choice   **2 cups grated Gruyère or other cheese of your choice**

OPTIONAL TOPPINGS

Ham and mustard   **Arugula, white Cheddar, and truffle oil**

Pop the bread in the toaster while you grate the cheese and preheat the broiler. Top the toasted bread with the cheese (or whatever other toppings you like—put them on the toast before you add the cheese) and broil until the cheese has melted and is starting to brown.

EASY TOMATO SOUP

Gluten-free, Under 30 minutes
SERVES 4

I love making tomato soup with garden tomatoes I've slow-roasted all day and homemade chicken stock that has been simmering on the stove for hours. But as a busy mom, it's hard to find the time (especially during the week!), which is why I came up with this quick-and-easy recipe. Ready in under 30 minutes, and very popular with the kids, this is in steady rotation at my house.

2 tablespoons olive oil

2 tablespoons unsalted butter

1 large onion, thinly sliced

½ teaspoon kosher salt, plus more to taste

3 garlic cloves, thinly sliced

3 tablespoons tomato paste

5 large fresh basil leaves

1 (28-ounce) can whole tomatoes with their juice

2 cups chicken stock

Freshly ground black pepper

¼ cup cream (optional)

(Continued)

Heat the olive oil and butter in a heavy-bottomed saucepan or Dutch oven over medium heat. Add the onion and salt; cover the pot and cook for 10 minutes. Add the garlic, tomato paste, and basil leaves and sauté for 2 minutes. Add the canned tomatoes and juice—breaking the tomatoes up with a wooden spoon—and the chicken stock. Bring the mixture to a boil, reduce to a simmer, and cook for 20 minutes. Using an immersion blender, blend the soup directly in the pot (alternatively, carefully transfer the soup in batches to a blender). Season with salt and pepper and stir in the cream, if desired.

PITA BREAD PIZZAS

Vegetarian, Under 30 minutes
SERVES 4

You know those nights when you're exhausted, your kids are hungry, and even the thought of picking up Chinese food makes you tired? One such night, while desperately searching through the fridge for something that could pass as dinner, I found whole wheat pita, some shredded mozzarella cheese, and a storage container with leftover tomato sauce. We sliced up some red onion, popped open a jar of olives, and grabbed some spicy chili flakes and fresh Parmesan cheese, and the pita bread pizza was born! It's easy, relatively healthy, and an undisputed crowd-pleaser. In other words, everybody wins.

4 whole wheat pita breads

1 cup Basic Tomato Sauce (page 242) or store-bought

1 cup shredded mozzarella cheese

Other toppings of choice, such as olives, pepperoni, mushrooms, etc.

Preheat the oven to 450°F.

Place the pitas on a baking sheet and pop them in the oven for 10 minutes to crisp up.

Pull them out, add the tomato sauce, mozzarella, and other toppings, and return them to the oven for another 10 minutes, or until the cheese has melted and is beginning to brown.

Remove and serve.

CONGEE

Gluten-free
SERVES 4

Congee is a Chinese rice porridge traditionally eaten for breakfast, but we think it also makes a perfect lazy dinner. If it's too thick, loosen it up with a little water or stock until it reaches your preferred consistency. If it's too thin, simply cook it a bit longer—we like it to have the texture of a thick soup.

8 cups chicken stock

6 garlic cloves, very finely grated or minced (about 2 tablespoons)

1 (3-inch) piece fresh ginger, peeled and very finely grated or minced (about 3 tablespoons)

3 tablespoons toasted sesame oil, plus extra for garnish

2/3 cup jasmine rice

4 large pinches of salt

4 poached, fried, or 6-minute eggs (page 244)

4 tablespoons tamari, or to taste

6 scallions, thinly sliced

Furikake seasoning (page 251)

Chopped fresh cilantro, for garnish

Combine the stock, garlic, ginger, sesame oil, rice, and salt in a medium saucepan. Bring the mixture to a boil, partially cover, and simmer over very low heat for 30 to 40 minutes (until the rice begins to break down), stirring every 5 minutes or so to make sure it isn't sticking.

Just before the rice is finished, cook the eggs.

Divide the congee among four bowls and season with tamari and sesame oil to taste. Place an egg in each bowl and garnish with the scallions, furikake, and cilantro.

POKE BOWLS

Poke, a Hawaiian raw seafood salad, is having a moment in Los Angeles, and for good reason. *Poke* bowls are fresh, healthy, and super easy to put together. Make one for a quick solo dinner or have some friends over for a *poke* bowl buffet. All you need is cooked rice or quinoa, diced sushi-quality fish (get someone at the seafood counter to do this for you), some fresh veggies and herbs, and a quick soy-based sauce. Here are two of our favorite bowls and four of our favorite sauces, but you can dress these up with literally anything you like.

TUNA POKE BOWL

Gluten-free, Under 30 minutes
SERVES 1

½ cup cooked white or brown rice

¼ cup cooked edamame

⅓ cup diced sushi-grade tuna, cut into ½-inch pieces

¼ cup diced avocado

2 tablespoons sesame seeds

2 tablespoons sliced scallions

2 tablespoons thinly sliced shiso

2 tablespoons Furikake seasoning (page 251)

Ponzu sauce (page 82)

Place the rice in a bowl, top with the edamame, tuna, avocado, sesame seeds, scallions, shiso, and furikake, and pour the ponzu dressing over.

SALMON POKE BOWL

Gluten-free, Under 30 minutes
SERVES 1

½ cup zucchini and cucumber noodles

⅓ cup diced salmon

2 tablespoons chopped cilantro

¼ cup peeled and grated carrot

¼ cup edamame

2 tablespoons sliced scallions

2 tablespoons Furikake seasoning (page 251)

Wasabi sauce (page 82)

Place the zucchini and cucumber noodles in a bowl, top with the salmon, cilantro, carrot, edamame, scallions, and furikake, and pour the wasabi dressing over.

(Continued)

POKE BOWL SAUCES

To make the sauces below, whisk or stir the recipe ingredients together until blended.

CLASSIC

2 tablespoons tamari

1 tablespoon rice wine vinegar

1 teaspoon toasted sesame oil

PONZU

2 tablespoons ponzu

1 tablespoon fresh lemon juice

WASABI

2 tablespoons tamari

1 tablespoon rice wine vinegar

½ teaspoon wasabi powder

SPICY MAYO

2 tablespoons Vegenaise

1 teaspoon toasted sesame oil

1 teaspoon sriracha

SESAME NOODLES

Vegan, Under 30 minutes
SERVES 4

Sesame, tamari, and noodles? Yes, please! I could eat the whole bowl. Great on their own, these noodles are even better topped with raw, steamed, or grilled veggies, tofu, or any cooked protein. We usually use soba because we like the nutty flavor of buckwheat, but you can use rice noodles, udon, or even spaghetti.

¾ **pound noodles of your choice**

⅓ **cup tamari**

3 **tablespoons mirin**

3 **tablespoons toasted sesame oil**

3 **scallions, thinly sliced**

Salt (optional)

Furikake seasoning (page 251)

Cook the noodles according to the package directions.

While the pasta cooks, whisk together the tamari, mirin, and sesame oil in a large bowl. When the noodles are ready, drain them and add directly to the bowl with the sauce; toss to combine. Let cool for about 10 minutes, then add the scallions and a little salt, if desired.

Serve with furikake on the side.

SHRIMP STIR-FRY

Gluten-free, Under 30 minutes
SERVES 4

Next time you're craving Chinese, try this recipe instead of ordering in. It's way healthier, you can make it in less time than delivery would take, and you won't be suffering from sodium bloat the next day. This makes a lot of sauce, so serve it over steamed rice or Sesame Noodles (page 83).

FOR THE SAUCE

¼ cup tamari

2 tablespoons brown rice syrup

1 tablespoon toasted sesame oil

1 teaspoon sambal oelek or your favorite hot sauce

2 teaspoons cornstarch

FOR THE STIR-FRY

2 tablespoons peanut or safflower oil

1 pound shrimp, peeled and deveined

1 (2-inch) piece fresh ginger, peeled and minced

2 large garlic cloves, minced

½ pound snow peas

5 large scallions, white parts halved lengthwise and cut into 1-inch pieces, green parts thinly sliced

To make the sauce, whisk together the ingredients in a medium bowl and set aside.

To make the stir-fry, heat the oil in a wok or large sauté pan over high heat. When the oil is very hot but not smoking, add the shrimp. Add the ginger and garlic and cook for 1 minute more, or until the shrimp are beginning to brown and the ginger and garlic smell fragrant. Add the snow peas and the white parts of the scallions and cook for a minute more, stirring to make sure the ingredients cook evenly.

Add the sauce and cook for about 2 minutes, stirring occasionally—it should begin to thicken immediately. When the sauce has thickened and the shrimp are cooked through, throw in the sliced scallion greens and serve.

TAQUITOS

Gluten-free
SERVES 4

My kids know to hide their plates from me on taquito night because I really can't be trusted—these little corn tortillas, stuffed with lightly seasoned chicken or black beans, rolled up tight, and baked in the oven until crispy, just might be my favorite food. Quickly frying each tortilla in oil, filling, and rolling does take some time, but since the filling is easy to make and I always have the ingredients on hand, they are so worth the effort. Serve with rice, beans, and Corn with Lime Butter (page 140) on the side. I've also served these as appetizers at a dinner party, and let's just say I'm not the only grown-up who can't resist them.

CHICKEN VERSION

1½ cups finely chopped cooked chicken (about ¼-inch pieces)

1 cup shredded Mexican cheese blend

2 tablespoons finely chopped fresh cilantro

½ teaspoon ground cumin

3 tablespoons finely diced white onion

Salt

BLACK BEAN VERSION

1 (14-ounce) can black beans, drained and rinsed

1 cup Mexican shredded cheese blend

2 tablespoons finely chopped fresh cilantro

½ teaspoon ground cumin

2 tablespoons finely diced white onion

Salt

Cooking spray

Olive oil or neutral oil, for frying

8 corn tortillas for the black bean version; or 12 for the chicken version

Fresh salsa (pages 254, 256, and 257), hot sauce, and/or guacamole, for serving

Preheat the oven to 400ºF. Lightly grease a baking sheet with cooking spray.

To make the chicken version, combine the chicken, cheese, cilantro, cumin, and onion in a large bowl and season with salt to taste.

To make the black bean version, combine the black beans, cheese, cilantro, cumin, and onion in a large bowl and season with salt to taste.

In a small sauté pan, heat about 1 tablespoon of oil over medium-high heat and quickly fry 1 tortilla (about 30 seconds on each side). Fill the softened tortilla with about 3 tablespoons of the chicken or black bean mixture, roll it up carefully, and place it seam side down on the prepared baking sheet. Continue frying, filling, and rolling the taquitos until you've used all the filling, then bake in the oven for 20 minutes.

Serve with salsas, hot sauce, and/or guacamole.

ZUCCHINI CACIO E PEPE

Vegetarian, Gluten-free, Under 30 minutes
SERVES 4

Cacio e pepe is one of my favorite simple pasta dishes, so when Thea and I started spiralizing vegetables like maniacs, we thought a zucchini noodle version might be nice. We were right—it's even more delicious than the original and so simple to make. If you don't already own a spiralizer, put this book down and order one. Now. Seriously, it will change your life.

3 medium zucchini, spiralized

¼ cup olive oil

1 teaspoon freshly ground black pepper

1 cup finely grated Parmesan cheese

Salt

In a large bowl, toss the zucchini noodles with the olive oil and pepper. Add the cheese, toss to combine, and season with salt to taste.

COZY EVENINGS

As the days get shorter and the weather gets colder, everybody craves cozy, comforting food for dinner. And while comfort food is often associated with hours-long preparations and lots of rich, heavy dishes, some of the most soothing food is the cleanest and simplest to prepare. There's nothing more warming on a rainy day than a steaming bowl of chicken wonton soup or a platter of creamy polenta with sautéed mushrooms. Whether eaten curled up in front of the TV or around the dining table, this is food that warms the body and the soul.

CANDIED KABOCHA SQUASH

Vegan, Gluten-free
SERVES 4

Kabocha is a round Japanese squash that seems to be steadily gaining popularity in the States. Its flesh, which is a little less sweet than butternut, has an almost starchy texture and wonderful nutty flavor. Roasting it with coconut oil and maple syrup until sticky and caramelized makes this a vegetable dish that even kids will devour. It is so delicious. I prefer to peel the skin, but if you're in a rush, it's fine to skip this step.

**1 (3-pound) kabocha squash,
peeled**

2 tablespoons coconut oil, melted

½ teaspoon kosher salt

2 tablespoons maple syrup

**1 teaspoon finely chopped fresh
rosemary (about 1 small sprig)**

Preheat the oven to 400°F.

Cut the squash in half, scoop out the seeds, and cut each half into 8 pieces.

Toss the squash with the remaining ingredients on a baking sheet and roast for 30 minutes, or until caramelized and tender.

CAULIFLOWER MAC 'N' CHEESE

Vegetarian
SERVES 6 TO 8

Okay, so mac 'n' cheese is not exactly a healthy dinner, but we can't be virtuous all the time! Plus, I managed to sneak in a whole head of cauliflower without any objections, so I'm not feeling too guilty. If it's easier, make this dish up to a day in advance and store it in the fridge until you need it. Just add about 10 minutes to the cooking time.

Cooking spray

Salt

5 tablespoons unsalted butter

¼ cup plus 1 tablespoon all-purpose flour

2 teaspoons minced fresh thyme leaves

4 cups whole milk

1 garlic clove, very finely grated or minced

A pinch of cayenne pepper

A pinch of ground nutmeg

½ pound Gruyère cheese, grated

½ pound white Cheddar cheese, grated

Freshly ground black pepper

1 pound elbow macaroni

1 small head of cauliflower, broken into small florets (cut any large florets into roughly ¾-inch pieces)

1 cup grated Parmesan cheese

½ cup panko bread crumbs

2 tablespoons olive oil

Preheat the oven to 375°F. Grease a 9 × 11-inch baking dish with cooking spray. Bring a large pot of salted water to a boil for the pasta.

Meanwhile, in a large saucepan or Dutch oven, melt the butter over medium heat. Add the flour and thyme and cook, stirring with a wooden spoon, for 2 minutes. Add the milk, ½ cup at a time, and cook until the mixture is thick enough to coat the wooden spoon, about 10 minutes. Add the garlic, cayenne, nutmeg, and 1½ packed cups each of the Gruyère and the white Cheddar; season with salt and pepper to taste.

Once the sauce is ready, add the pasta to the boiling water and cook for 5 minutes. Add the cauliflower and cook for 1 minute more. Drain the pasta, toss it with the cheese sauce, and pour the mixture into the prepared baking dish.

In a medium bowl, combine the remaining Gruyère and Cheddar, the Parmesan, panko, and olive oil and season with a pinch of salt. Spread the mixture evenly over the mac 'n' cheese and bake for 30 minutes, or until the topping is brown and crispy and the cheese sauce is bubbling.

CHICKEN AND ZUCCHINI NOODLE PHO

Gluten-free, Under 30 minutes
SERVES 2

I developed this recipe for a GOOP story we did highlighting our then new and still favorite kitchen tool, the spiralizer. GP was dubious at first—pho without rice noodles sounds like kind of a bummer—but when she downed the whole bowl and asked if there was any more, I knew we had a winner. Feel free to use leftover shredded chicken or skip it altogether, but don't forget to infuse the stock with ginger, garlic, and cilantro for great depth of flavor. —TB

4 cups chicken stock

1 bone-in, skin-on chicken breast

8 sprigs fresh cilantro

1 (3-inch) piece fresh ginger, sliced

3 garlic cloves, smashed

Salt

1 tablespoon maple syrup

1 tablespoon tamari

½ small white onion, very thinly sliced

Juice of 1 lime

1 zucchini, spiralized

TO SERVE

8 sprigs fresh cilantro

4 sprigs fresh basil

1 small serrano chili, sliced

A handful of mung bean sprouts

1 lime, quartered

Combine the chicken stock, chicken, cilantro, ginger, garlic, a large pinch of salt, and 2 cups water in a medium saucepan; the chicken should be just covered by the liquid. Bring the liquid to a boil, reduce the heat to maintain a simmer, and poach the chicken for 10 to 15 minutes, or until completely cooked through.

Remove the chicken breast, shred the meat, and return the carcass to the saucepan. Simmer on low for 10 minutes. Strain the stock, discarding the solids, and return it to the saucepan. Add the maple syrup, tamari, onion, and lime juice. Taste for seasoning and add salt, if desired.

Divide the spiralized zucchini and shredded chicken between two bowls. Ladle over the hot liquid, and serve with the fresh herbs, chili, sprouts, and lime wedges on the side.

CHICKEN ENCHILADAS

SERVES 4 TO 6

There is almost nothing more satisfying than a bubbling casserole dish filled with cheesy chicken enchiladas, and these do not disappoint. The chipotle peppers add a spicy, smoky element to the sauce, and the Mexican oregano imparts a touch of traditional flavor. The sauce does take a little time, so make a double batch on a Sunday and freeze half (or skip it and use a good canned enchilada sauce—we won't tell).

Cooking spray or olive oil

FOR THE SAUCE

1 medium yellow onion, roughly chopped

½ cup packed roughly chopped fresh cilantro

3 large garlic cloves, smashed

3 tablespoons olive oil

½ teaspoon ground coriander

½ teaspoon chili powder

1 teaspoon ground cumin

¾ teaspoon salt

1 (28-ounce) can diced tomatoes with juice

2 chipotles in adobo, plus 4 teaspoons adobo sauce from the can

FOR THE ENCHILADAS

4 cups shredded chicken (from about 1 rotisserie chicken)

1 teaspoon Mexican oregano

½ small white onion, very thinly sliced

1 cup shredded cheese (Cheddar, mozzarella, or Mexican blend)

1 cup crumbled queso fresco

Salt

8 spelt or flour tortillas

Preheat the oven to 375°F. Grease a 9 × 11-inch baking dish with cooking spray or olive oil.

To make the sauce, combine the onion, cilantro, and garlic in the bowl of a food processor and process for 7 seconds. Scrape down the sides of the bowl with a spatula and blend for another 7 seconds, until very finely chopped and almost smooth.

Heat the olive oil in a large sauté pan or Dutch oven over medium-high heat. Add the onion mixture, the coriander, chili powder, cumin, and salt and cook for 5 minutes, or until the liquid has evaporated and the mixture starts to brown.

Meanwhile, in a food processor, combine the tomatoes, chipotles, and adobo sauce and process until smooth.

Pour the tomato mixture into the pan with the onion mixture, bring to a boil, then reduce the heat to maintain a simmer and cook for 10 minutes more.

To make the enchiladas, in a bowl, combine the shredded chicken, oregano, onion, ½ cup of the shredded cheese, and ½ cup of the crumbled queso fresco. When the sauce is ready, add 1½ cups to the chicken mixture and stir to combine. Taste the filling and add salt if necessary (some rotisseried chickens are saltier than others).

Pour half the remaining sauce into the prepared baking dish, using a spatula to spread it evenly over the bottom of the dish. Place one spelt or flour tortilla on a flat surface, fill it with one-eighth of the chicken mixture, carefully roll it up, and place it seam side down in the baking dish. Repeat with the remaining tortillas and filling, then pour the remaining sauce over the top, using a spatula to spread evenly.

Cover the dish with aluminum foil and bake for 15 minutes. Remove the foil, sprinkle the remaining ½ cup shredded cheese and ½ cup queso fresco evenly over the enchiladas, and return to the oven for 10 to 15 minutes, or until the cheese has melted and the sauce is bubbling.

Finish the enchiladas under the broiler to brown the cheese, if desired.

CHICKEN WONTON SOUP

SERVES 4

Everyone loves wonton soup, but who has time to fold up individual dumplings for a midweek dinner? In this deconstructed recipe, we keep the wrappers and the filling, but ditch the arduous dumpling assembly step. The result? All the flavor of a good wonton soup without all the fuss. These chicken meatballs are addictive. We sometimes skip the soup part, bake or pan-fry the meatballs, and serve them with Sesame Noodles (page 83) or Cauliflower and Kimchi "Fried Rice" (page 179).

FOR THE SOUP

8 cups chicken stock

2 large scallions, cut into 2-inch pieces

2 garlic cloves, smashed

1 (3-inch) piece fresh ginger, cut into ¼-inch slices

A pinch of salt

FOR THE MEATBALLS

1 pound ground dark meat chicken

4 small scallions, minced or finely chopped

2 heaping tablespoons finely chopped fresh cilantro

2 teaspoons very finely grated or minced fresh ginger

1 teaspoon toasted sesame oil

4 teaspoons tamari

½ teaspoon kosher salt

4 baby bok choy, cut into quarters

¼ pound snow peas, strings removed

20 square wonton wrappers, cut into ½-inch strips

To make the soup, combine the chicken stock, scallions, garlic, ginger, and salt in a pot or Dutch oven. Bring the mixture to a boil, then reduce the heat to maintain a low simmer, cover, and allow the flavors to infuse while you prepare the meatballs.

To make the meatballs, in a medium bowl, mix together all the meatball ingredients, making sure everything is evenly combined. Wet your hands so the mixture doesn't stick, and roll into 24 small meatballs.

To finish the soup, remove the aromatics from the broth (either by straining or pulling them out with tongs), add the meatballs, and simmer for 5 minutes, or until cooked through. Add the bok choy, snow peas, and wonton wrappers and simmer for 1 minute more before serving.

GINGER CARROT SOUP

Gluten-free
SERVES 4

This ubiquitous combo has been around for ages, popping up at spas, restaurants, and even the canned soup aisle at the supermarket. I've had a million iterations of this soup, but our version, naturally sweet from slowly sautéed onion and bright with lots of fresh ginger, is particularly good (and easy!). Don't bother peeling the carrots for this recipe—just give them a good scrub to remove any dirt.

2 tablespoons coconut oil

1 large onion, cut in half and thinly sliced

Salt

2 garlic cloves, thinly sliced

2 tablespoons chopped fresh ginger

1 teaspoon ground cumin

½ teaspoon ground coriander

½ teaspoon garam masala

1 pound carrots, cut into 1-inch pieces (about 2½ cups)

3 cups chicken or vegetable stock

Freshly ground black pepper

Heat the coconut oil in a heavy-bottomed saucepan over medium heat. Add the onion and a pinch of salt, cover the pot, and sauté over low heat for about 20 minutes, until the onion is very soft and sweet.

Add the garlic and ginger, sauté for 1 minute, then add the cumin, coriander, and garam masala. Sauté for another minute, then add the carrots, stock, and another big pinch of salt. Bring the mixture to a boil, then turn down the heat and simmer gently for about 20 minutes, or until the carrots are very tender.

Carefully transfer the soup in batches to a high-speed blender, or blend the soup directly in the pot with an immersion blender. Season to taste with salt and pepper.

INDIAN CREAMED SPINACH

Vegetarian, Gluten-free, Under 30 minutes
SERVES 4 TO 6

My favorite thing about steak houses might be creamed spinach, and my favorite thing about Indian restaurants is definitely saag paneer. Here's a recipe that marries the two, blending the comforting texture of creamed spinach with the wonderful spices of saag paneer. A great side dish, it also makes a super-satisfying vegetarian main course, served simply with store-bought naan or over a steaming bowl of basmati rice. —TB

2 tablespoons olive oil

2 tablespoons unsalted butter

1 large or 2 medium onions, roughly chopped

6 garlic cloves, minced

1 (4-inch) piece fresh ginger, peeled and minced (about 3 tablespoons)

1 teaspoon garam masala

½ teaspoon ground coriander

1 teaspoon ground cumin

1 (16-ounce) package frozen chopped spinach, thawed, excess moisture squeezed out

1 teaspoon salt

½ cup whole milk yogurt

¼ cup heavy cream

In a Dutch oven or similar pot, heat the oil and butter over medium-high heat. Add the onion, garlic, and ginger, reduce the heat to medium, and sauté for 10 minutes, or until the onion starts to brown. Add the garam masala, coriander, and cumin and sauté for 2 minutes more. Stir in the spinach, salt, and ½ cup water, reduce the heat to low, cover, and cook for 3 minutes, or until the spinach is heated through.

Turn off the heat, stir in the yogurt and heavy cream, and use an immersion blender to blend the mixture directly in the pot until almost completely smooth.

MISO CLAMS

Gluten-free, Under 30 minutes

SERVES 4

An impressive and easy one-pot meal with seven simple ingredients—what more could you want? This makes a lot of cooking liquid, so we like to serve it in shallow bowls over rice or with toasted bread on the side to sop up the ginger-laced juices. Because the miso is salty, look for the smallest, sweetest clams you can find, and be sure to clean them really well.*

6 large garlic cloves, thinly sliced

1 (5-inch) piece fresh ginger, peeled and thinly sliced

3 cups sake

3 pounds small clams, such as manila or littleneck, cleaned

4 tablespoons (½ stick) unsalted butter

4 tablespoons white miso, dissolved in 3 tablespoons very hot water

6 scallions, thinly sliced

Combine the garlic, ginger, and sake in a heavy-bottomed saucepan or Dutch oven and bring to a simmer. Cook for 5 to 10 minutes, until the aromatics have flavored the sake and most of the alcohol has cooked off.

Add the clams, cover the pot, and cook for about 5 minutes, or until the shells start to open; add the butter and miso and stir to dissolve.

Garnish with the scallions and serve.

* My friend Elouisa has figured out the best way to clean clams. First, she fills a bowl with cold water and lets the clams soak for about 10 minutes. Then she drains them, sprinkles them with a handful of coarse salt, and scrubs the clams against themselves, picking them up by the handful and rubbing them together. She does this hard enough to get any and all dirt off, but with a soft enough touch so as not to break the shells. She rinses them, soaks them in cold water again, and then drains them when the pan is ready for them. The cleanest clams I know.

MISO TURNIPS

Vegetarian, Gluten-free, Under 30 minutes
SERVES 4

So good, I could eat a whole pound of these. Be sure to watch the turnips carefully while they're under the broiler—you want them to brown and caramelize, but not burn. If you can't find little white Tokyo turnips, use whatever variety they have at the grocery store—just be sure to peel them (the skin of larger turnips can be quite bitter) and cut them into 1-inch pieces.

1 pound Tokyo turnips, small ones left whole and larger ones cut in half, or regular turnips, peeled and cut into 1-inch pieces

Olive oil

Salt

1 tablespoon unsalted butter

1 tablespoon white miso paste

1 tablespoon maple syrup

2 tablespoons toasted sesame seeds (optional)

Preheat the oven to 425°F.

Toss the turnips with olive oil and salt on a rimmed baking sheet and roast for 15 to 20 minutes.

Meanwhile, in a small saucepan, melt together the butter, miso, and maple syrup over medium heat.

Coat the turnips with the miso mixture and broil until beginning to brown, 3 to 5 minutes.

Garnish with toasted sesame seeds, if desired.

PAN-SEARED BRUSSELS SPROUTS

Vegan, Gluten-free, Under 30 minutes
SERVES 4

I can get down with a jazzed-up Brussels sprout (who doesn't love them deep-fried with a sweet glaze and crispy bacon?), but sometimes I crave a simpler preparation. In this recipe, thinly sliced sprouts (a food processor with the slicing blade attachment takes care of this task in minutes) are quickly sautéed in good olive oil until crispy and sizzling, then tossed with a hint of garlic and a good pinch of sea salt. That's it, and it's glorious. Add more oil as necessary to keep things cooking evenly, and try adding a squeeze of lemon and a pinch of chili flakes just before serving.

¼ cup olive oil

4 cups shaved Brussels sprouts (about 1 pound)

2 large garlic cloves, very finely grated or minced

Salt and freshly ground black pepper

Lemon juice (optional)

Chili flakes (optional)

Heat a large sauté pan over high heat. Add the olive oil and shaved Brussels sprouts in an even layer; let sit untouched until the bottom layer begins to brown and smell crispy. Shake the pan or use a wooden spoon to stir every so often so that most of the sprouts get nicely browned. Add the garlic, stir to combine with the sprouts, and cook for 30 seconds, or until fragrant. Season generously with salt and black pepper and serve with a squeeze of lemon juice and some chili flakes, if desired.

CRISPY POLENTA WITH SAUCE

Vegetarian, Gluten-free
SERVES 4

There's a great Italian restaurant near my house in Los Angeles called Giorgio Baldi, and whenever I take my kids there, they order crispy polenta with tomato sauce. Here's my version, spiced up with a little rosemary and chili.

1 cup instant polenta

1 tablespoon chopped fresh rosemary

A pinch of chili flakes

1 garlic clove, very finely grated or minced

½ cup grated Parmesan cheese, plus more for serving

Salt and freshly ground black pepper

Olive oil for greasing the baking dish, plus more as needed

Basic Tomato Sauce (page 242) or your favorite jarred tomato sauce

Cook the polenta on the stovetop according to the package directions, then stir in the rosemary, chili flakes, garlic, and cheese. Season to taste with salt and pepper and pour into a greased 8 × 8-inch baking dish. Let cool slightly, then refrigerate for at least 1 hour to set.

When ready to serve, invert the baking dish onto a cutting board. Cut the polenta into 12 squares and either sear in a nonstick pan with olive oil or grill until crispy. Serve with warm tomato sauce and freshly grated Parmesan cheese.

RAMEN

A good bowl of ramen is a beautiful thing, and I've been lucky enough to have had many over the years. On a recent trip to New York, I had a particularly mind-blowing bowl at Ramen Lab and came back to L.A. raving about it. Realizing that ramen would be a great addition to this book, Thea and I set to work developing some quick-and-easy recipes inspired by some of our favorite shops. These can all be made in 30 minutes or less (except for the pork belly, which takes some time, but is totally worth it), but taste like you've been slaving for hours.

MISO RAMEN

Vegetarian, Under 30 minutes
SERVES 4

The red miso, soy, and dried mushrooms give this vegetarian broth incredible flavor.

¼ cup red miso paste

¼ cup tamari

24 dried shiitake mushrooms

4 small or 2 large garlic cloves, very finely grated or minced

12 ounces ramen noodles, cooked and drained

8 fresh shiitake mushrooms, thinly sliced

8 baby bok choy, thinly sliced

4 scallions, thinly sliced, for garnish

Four 6-minute eggs (page 244), halved, for serving

Combine the miso, tamari, dried mushrooms, garlic, and 8 cups water in a large saucepan and bring to a boil; reduce the heat to maintain a simmer while you prepare the bowls.

Divide the noodles among four large bowls, then top with the fresh shiitake mushrooms and bok choy. Remove the dried mushrooms from the broth, pour the broth over the noodles, and garnish with sliced scallions. Finish each bowl with a soft-boiled egg.

SPRING VEGGIE RAMEN

Vegetarian, Under 30 minutes
SERVES 4

Ramen Shop in Oakland, started by some Chez Panisse alums, serves a vegetarian ramen that changed my life. It's full of Meyer lemon zest and is so bright and fresh, it's crazy. Here's our spring veggie recipe, inspired by them. —TB

1 tablespoon plus 1 teaspoon very finely grated fresh ginger

½ cup tamari

12 ounces ramen noodles, cooked and drained

20 snap peas, cut into ½-inch slices

8 fresh shiitake mushrooms, thinly sliced

12 baby bok choy, cut into 1-inch pieces

2 teaspoons lemon zest, for garnish

4 scallions, thinly sliced, for garnish

Four 6-minute eggs (page 244), halved, for serving

Combine the ginger, ponzu, and 8 cups water in a large saucepan and bring to a boil. Reduce the heat and simmer gently while you prepare the bowls.

Divide the noodles among four bowls and top with the snap peas, mushrooms, and bok choy. Pour the broth over the noodles, then finish each bowl with ½ teaspoon of the fresh lemon zest, sliced scallions, and a soft-boiled egg.

SPICY SHRIMP RAMEN

Under 30 minutes
SERVES 4

Dashi is a magic ingredient, made from bonito and soy, which gives you an intensely flavorful broth instantly. Look for it in the soy aisle at most Asian supermarkets.

¾ cup dashi

24 dried shiitake mushrooms

16 large shell-on shrimp

12 ounces ramen noodles (or whatever you can find), cooked and drained

8 small or 4 large fresh shiitake mushrooms, stemmed and thinly sliced

1 cup sliced baby bok choy

Four 6-minute eggs (page 244), halved, for serving

4 scallions, thinly sliced

1 jalapeño, thinly sliced

Furikake seasoning (page 251)

Combine the dashi, dried shiitakes, and 8 cups water in a large saucepan over medium-high heat. Bring to a boil, then reduce the heat and simmer for 5 minutes; remove the shiitakes, reduce the heat to very low, add the shrimp, cover, and poach in the hot liquid while you prepare the bowls, about 5 minutes.

Divide the noodles, fresh shiitake mushrooms, and bok choy among four bowls. Divide the shrimp and broth among them, then top each bowl with an egg, sliced scallion, sliced jalapeño, and furikake.

RAMEN WITH ROASTED PORK

SERVES 4

If you don't have time to cook the pork belly, this ramen is still delicious without.

¾ pound skinless pork belly, cut into 4 pieces

1 teaspoon salt

1 teaspoon coconut sugar

8 cups chicken stock

¾ cup dashi

12 ounces ramen noodles, cooked and drained

8 fresh shiitake mushrooms, stemmed and thinly sliced

4 scallions, thinly sliced

Four 6-minute eggs (page 244), halved, for serving

½ cup bonito flakes

Preheat the oven to 325°F. Rub the pork belly with the salt and sugar and place it in a small baking dish just large enough to hold it comfortably. Roast the pork belly for 45 minutes, basting it with its rendered fat every 10 minutes or so, until the meat is tender and beautifully browned. Remove from the oven and let rest for 5 minutes before thinly slicing.

Meanwhile, in a large saucepan, bring the chicken stock and dashi to a boil.

Divide the noodles among four bowls, then top with the sliced mushrooms and sliced pork. Pour in the dashi broth and finish with the scallions, soft-boiled eggs, and bonito flakes.

RAPINI PASTA
WITH GARLIC AND ANCHOVIES

Under 30 minutes
SERVES 6

I can't get enough of the bitter, complex flavor of rapini, or broccoli rabe as it's often called. I love it simply sautéed with lots of salt and garlic, and I recently learned to enjoy it raw (see our Brussels Sprouts and Rapini Salad, page 174), but I especially love it in this simple pasta, which I have been making variations of for years. Since all the other ingredients are staples most cooks keep on hand, buy the next beautiful bunch of rapini you spot and give this recipe a go. You won't regret it. —TB

Salt

3 tablespoons olive oil

3 anchovies

4 garlic cloves, thinly sliced

A pinch of chili flakes

1 pound orecchiette, or your favorite pasta shape

1 large bunch rapini (broccoli rabe), roughly chopped

Zest of 1 lemon

½ cup grated Parmesan cheese, plus extra for serving

Freshly ground black pepper

Bring a pot of heavily salted water to a boil for the pasta.

Meanwhile, in a very large sauté pan, heat the oil and anchovies over medium heat, stirring with a wooden spoon until the anchovies have melted. Add the garlic and chili flakes and cook until the garlic begins to sizzle and is fragrant, about 1 minute; turn off the heat.

Cook the pasta according to the package instructions until al dente, adding the rapini 1 minute before the pasta is finished. Reserve 1 cup of the pasta cooking water, then drain the pasta and rapini and add them to the sauté pan along with the lemon zest and Parmesan. Return the pan to medium heat and toss everything together, adding the reserved pasta water a bit at a time, until you achieve a nice light sauce. Season with salt and pepper to taste, and serve with extra grated Parmesan.

ROASTED CAULIFLOWER
WITH CURRY AND LIME

Vegan, Gluten-free, Under 30 minutes
SERVES 4

Roasting cauliflower at such a high temperature gives it great flavor, and the mix of curry powder, lime juice, Vegenaise, and fresh cilantro yields maximum flavor with minimal effort.

2 medium heads cauliflower, cut into large bite-sized pieces

½ teaspoon curry powder

A pinch of salt

2 tablespoons olive oil

3 tablespoons Vegenalse

Juice of 1 lime

3 tablespoons chopped fresh cilantro

Preheat the oven to 450ºF.

Put the cauliflower florets on a baking sheet and toss with the curry powder, salt, and olive oil. Roast for 20 minutes, or until just beginning to brown and crisp up.

While the cauliflower roasts, mix the Vegenaise and lime juice in a large bowl. When the cauliflower comes out of the oven, toss it in the bowl with the Vegenaise mixture and add the cilantro. Mix everything together, taste for seasoning, and serve.

SOFT POLENTA WITH SAUTÉED MUSHROOMS

Vegetarian, Gluten-free, Under 30 minutes
SERVES 4

Earthy mushrooms and creamy polenta are a match made in culinary heaven. Be sure to buy good-quality truffle oil—we learned that the majority of what's on the market is created by perfumers and actually contains no truffles.

FOR THE POLENTA

1 teaspoon salt	1/3 cup grated Parmesan cheese
1 cup instant polenta	2 tablespoons unsalted butter

FOR THE MUSHROOMS

2 tablespoons olive oil	2 small garlic cloves, minced
2 tablespoons unsalted butter	2 teaspoons white truffle oil
6 cups sliced assorted mushrooms (such as cremini, shiitake, oyster, chanterelle, morel)	Salt and freshly ground black pepper
2 tablespoons chopped fresh sage leaves	
Coarse sea salt, for serving	Grated Parmesan cheese, for serving

In a medium saucepan, bring 3 cups water plus the salt to a boil.

While the polenta water heats up, start the mushrooms: Heat the olive oil and butter in a large sauté pan over medium-high heat. When the butter has melted, add the mushrooms and cook for 3 minutes, stirring occasionally, until they have released their juices and are starting to brown. Add the sage and garlic and cook for 2 minutes more. Add the truffle oil and salt and pepper to taste.

Meanwhile, add the polenta to the boiling water and cook according to the package instructions. Add the Parmesan and butter and transfer to a serving platter or bowl. Top with the sautéed mushrooms, coarse sea salt, and extra Parmesan.

TURKEY MEAT LOAF

Gluten-free
SERVES 4 (WITH LEFTOVERS)

This makes a lot of meat loaf, but it's so good that people usually go in for seconds (or thirds), and the leftovers reheat beautifully. I learned to place a loaf pan or baking dish of water in the bottom of the oven when making cheesecake, and I employ the same method here. Apparently it keeps things moist and helps ensure that the cheesecake (or meat loaf, in this case) doesn't crack. Might be an old wives' tale, but this meat loaf comes out moist and delicious every time. —TB

4 ounces turkey bacon, roughly chopped

1 medium yellow onion, roughly chopped

2 large garlic cloves, roughly chopped

2 teaspoons fresh thyme leaves

2 tablespoons olive oil

½ cup gluten-free rolled oats

½ cup whole milk

3 tablespoons Worcestershire sauce

2 tablespoons plus ¼ cup ketchup

2½ teaspoons salt

1 large egg

Freshly cracked black pepper

2 pounds ground dark turkey meat

Preheat the oven to 375°F.

Combine the turkey bacon, onion, garlic, and thyme in the bowl of a food processor. Process until minced but stop before the mixture becomes a paste.

Heat the olive oil in a large sauté pan over medium-high heat. Add the onion mixture and cook for 6 to 8 minutes, or until slightly browned and fragrant. Set aside to cool.

While the onion mixture cools, in a large bowl, combine the oats, milk, Worcestershire, 2 tablespoons of the ketchup, the salt, egg, and pepper to taste and mix well with your hands.

Add the sautéed onion mixture and the ground turkey and mix until everything is evenly incorporated. At this stage, the mixture looks quite wet—don't worry, it will firm up in the oven.

Place the meat loaf on a parchment paper–lined baking sheet and shape it into a rounded rectangle. Brush the top with the remaining ¼ cup ketchup and bake for 45 minutes (place a small pan of water on the bottom oven rack to keep the meat loaf moist).

SUMMER NIGHTS

Oh, the magic of summer nights. I'm lucky enough to spend summers on Long Island, where most meals are enjoyed around a large farmhouse table in the backyard. Because produce is bounteous and intensely flavorful this time of year (by August, the vegetable garden is bursting with a zillion varieties of tomatoes, zucchini, peppers, and tons of fresh herbs, among other things), I tend toward simple, healthy preparations that can be thrown together quickly and highlight the local ingredients, such as cherry tomatoes tossed with warm pasta, garlic, and lemon zest; grilled salmon skewers dunked in herb flecked yogurt sauce; and big family-style salads. Add some friends, a bottle of crisp white wine, and my kids, sun-kissed and still dripping with salty ocean water, and we have the definition of a summer night.

BO BUN SALAD

Gluten-free
SERVES 4

This Vietnamese salad is healthy, fresh, and gluten free—need we say more? The play of spicy, sweet, salty, and sour in the marinade creates incredible flavor and helps the meat caramelize beautifully on the grill—it's also really good on steak, shrimp, and tofu.

FOR THE CHICKEN

Zest and juice of 1 lime

¼ cup fish sauce

2 teaspoons coconut sugar

4 slices red jalapeño, with seeds

12 sprigs fresh cilantro, chopped

1 (2-inch) piece fresh ginger, sliced

2 boneless, skinless chicken breasts, cut in half horizontally to make 4 cutlets

2 tablespoons olive oil

FOR THE CRISPY SHALLOTS

1 cup peanut oil, for frying

3 shallots, thinly sliced

Salt

FOR THE DRESSING

½ cup fresh lime juice (from about 4 limes)

¼ cup fish sauce

2 tablespoons maple syrup

½ teaspoon very finely grated garlic

½ teaspoon very finely grated fresh ginger

A large pinch of chili flakes

TO ASSEMBLE

3 ounces rice noodles, softened in warm water

1 medium zucchini, spiralized

1 large carrot, peeled and spiralized

½ cup roughly chopped fresh basil, divided

½ cup roughly chopped fresh mint, divided

½ cup roughly chopped fresh cilantro, divided

2 cups finely shredded white cabbage or red-leaf or Little Gem lettuce

2 Armenian cucumbers, halved lengthwise, seeded, and cut into half-moons

To make the chicken, combine all the ingredients except the olive oil in a medium bowl and let the chicken marinate at room temperature for at least 20 minutes or up to 1 hour. You can also marinate the chicken overnight in the fridge.

To make the crispy shallots, heat the peanut oil in a sauté pan or small saucepan over medium-high heat. When the oil is hot but not smoking, add the shallots and fry for 2 minutes, until brown but not dark. Transfer to a paper towel–lined plate to drain and season with salt.

While the shallots drain, whisk together all the dressing ingredients in a medium bowl.

Heat a grill pan to medium-high and brush lightly with the olive oil. When the pan is very hot but not smoking, grill the chicken for 5 to 7 minutes on each side. Remove to a plate or cutting board and let rest 5 minutes before thinly slicing.

To assemble the salad, in a large bowl, toss together the rice noodles, zucchini, carrot, herbs, cabbage, and cucumbers. Divide the salad among four large bowls or transfer to a large platter. Top with the sliced grilled chicken and crispy shallots, and serve with the dressing on the side.

CAULIFLOWER TABBOULEH

Vegan, Gluten-free, Under 30 minutes
SERVES 4 TO 6 AS A SIDE DISH

Thea developed a couple of cauliflower "couscous" recipes while working on the annual GOOP detox this year, and I was instantly hooked. Pulse your cauliflower right before serving and eat it soon after—raw cauliflower is delicious and nutritious, but the sulfur compounds can let off an unpleasant odor if left for too long. If you can find purple, yellow, or green cauliflower, they make for an especially stunning presentation.

½ medium head of cauliflower

1 small garlic clove, very finely grated or minced

Juice of 1 small lemon, plus more to taste

¼ cup olive oil, plus more to taste

A pinch of Aleppo pepper

A pinch of salt, plus more to taste

About ½ English cucumber, seeded and cut into ½-inch pieces (1 cup)

⅓ cup chopped fresh parsley

⅓ cup chopped fresh mint

⅓ cup chopped fresh cilantro

2 scallions, thinly sliced

To make the cauliflower "couscous," break the cauliflower into florets, then pulse in a food processor 10 to 15 times for 1 to 2 seconds each time. Stop when the cauliflower has been broken down into pieces the size of quinoa or couscous.

In the bottom of your serving bowl, whisk together the garlic, lemon juice, olive oil, Aleppo pepper, and a pinch of salt. Add the cauliflower, cucumber, herbs, and scallions and toss to combine. Season with salt, more lemon juice, and olive oil to taste.

BBQ CHICKEN SKEWERS

Gluten-free

SERVES 4

You can't go wrong with BBQ chicken, and skewers make everything more fun. If your grocery store doesn't sell chicken tenders, cut up boneless, skinless chicken breasts into 1 × 4-inch strips. I like these with our BBQ Sauce, but if you don't have time to make it, use your favorite store-bought brand.

12 chicken tenders (about 2 pounds)

2 tablespoons olive oil

Salt and freshly ground black pepper

1 cup BBQ Sauce (page 243) or your favorite store-bought version, plus extra for serving

Soak 12 wooden skewers in water for 20 minutes.

Toss the chicken pieces with the olive oil, a couple of generous pinches of salt, and some pepper. Heat a grill pan over medium-high heat. Skewer each chicken tender individually.

Grill the skewers for 5 minutes on each side. Brush each one with 1 to 2 tablespoons of the sauce and cook for 3 more minutes, or until the chicken is cooked through and the sauce is beginning to brown and caramelize. When all the chicken is cooked, transfer the skewers to plates or a platter and serve with extra BBQ sauce on the side.

CHICKEN CHOW MEIN

Under 30 minutes

SERVES 4

It can be difficult to re-create favorite Chinese take-out dishes at home (maybe something about the insane amount of oil most restaurants use?), but this recipe is a real winner. And, with only six ingredients, it's a snap to pull together. I love my giant wok, but if you don't happen to have one, you may have to cook this chow mein in two batches—just be sure not to crowd the noodles.

9 ounces udon noodles or fettucine

6 tablespoons peanut oil

1 pound boneless, skinless chicken breast (about 2 breasts), cut into ¾ × 2-inch strips

Salt

1 bunch broccolini, cut into ½-inch pieces

1 large yellow onion, thinly sliced

⅓ cup tamari

Cook the udon noodles according to the package instructions; drain and rinse with cold water.

Heat a wok or very large nonstick sauté pan over high heat. Add 3 tablespoons of the peanut oil and arrange the chicken strips in one even layer around the pan; season the chicken with salt.

Sear the chicken for 2 minutes, or until nicely browned on one side; turn and sear on the second side, then transfer to a large bowl.

Add the broccolini to the wok and sauté, stirring frequently, for 3 to 5 minutes. Use a slotted spoon to transfer the broccolini to the bowl with the chicken, leaving as much oil in the wok as possible.

Add the onion to the wok and cook for 5 to 7 minutes, or until beginning to soften and caramelize, then add the remaining 3 tablespoons peanut oil and the cooked noodles. Stir the noodles and arrange them so that as many as possible are in direct contact with the pan (you want them to sear as much as possible) and cook for 1 minute. Return the chicken and broccolini to the wok, stir to combine everything, and cook for 3 minutes or so more. Add the tamari, turn off the heat, and serve.

CHICKEN PICCATA

Under 30 minutes
SERVES 4

Growing up, I struggled with the briny, sharply acidic flavors of this dish (which, unfortunately for me, was one of my dad's favorite things to cook), but now I can't get enough of it. If you're short on time, get someone at the meat counter to pound out your chicken for you and be sure to let the lemon slices get caramelized and sweet before adding the other ingredients. If you want dinner ready ASAP, and don't mind cleaning more dishes, use two sauté pans to cook all the chicken at once. —TB

2 pounds chicken cutlets, pounded to ¼-inch thickness

¼ cup all-purpose flour

4 tablespoons neutral oil, or as needed

Salt and freshly ground black pepper

1 lemon, cut into ¼-inch slices

¼ cup capers

4 tablespoons (½ stick) unsalted butter

Juice of 1 lemon

¼ cup finely chopped fresh parsley

Use a paper towel to dry the cutlets well and place the flour on a large plate or in a shallow bowl.

Meanwhile, heat the oil in a large sauté pan over medium-high heat, season the cutlets generously with salt and pepper, then dredge them, one at a time, in the flour before placing them in the hot sauté pan. Cook until nicely browned on one side, about 3 minutes, then flip and brown the other side.

When the chicken is nicely browned and cooked through, transfer it to a plate or serving platter and cover to keep warm. Repeat until all the chicken has been cooked (you will most likely have to do this in batches). Add the lemon slices to the pan, cooking until browned and slightly softened, 1 to 2 minutes. Reduce the heat to medium; add the capers, butter, lemon juice, and a large pinch of salt and cook for 1 minute.

Taste for seasoning, add the parsley, pour the sauce over the chicken, and serve.

CORN WITH LIME BUTTER

Vegetarian, Gluten-free, Under 30 minutes

SERVES 4

Butter and corn could not be a more perfect match, but even the classics need reinterpretation from time to time. Here we added a little lime zest and smoky chipotle powder to make things a bit more interesting. Great on steamed, roasted, or grilled corn, the lime butter is also delicious on roasted salmon and grilled steak, so you might want to make a double batch.

4 tablespoons (½ stick) salted butter, at room temperature

Zest of 1 lime

¼ teaspoon chipotle chili powder

4 ears of corn, husks and silk removed

Mix the butter, lime zest, and chipotle powder in a small bowl.

Steam, grill, or roast the corn. Slather it with the flavored butter and serve.

FALAFEL

Vegetarian, Gluten-free
MAKES ABOUT 30 SMALL FALAFEL

Most falafel recipes we've encountered involve soaking raw chickpeas overnight (which, let's be honest, isn't totally practical for a weeknight dinner), so we decided to develop our own quick version. It takes about 15 minutes to prep and 20 to cook. Make sandwiches with pita, chopped tomatoes, diced romaine, and our Cilantro Hummus (page 248) or serve over Spring Fattoush Salad (page 154) for a light supper.

Olive oil or cooking spray for the baking sheet

2 (15-ounce) cans chickpeas, drained and rinsed

10 sprigs fresh parsley, roughly chopped

10 sprigs fresh cilantro, roughly chopped

4 scallions, thinly sliced

3 garlic cloves, very finely grated or minced

1 teaspoon ground cumin

¼ teaspoon harissa powder, or ⅛ teaspoon cayenne pepper

¼ cup Greek yogurt

2 teaspoons salt, or to taste

Preheat the oven to 450°F. Grease a baking sheet.

In a food processor, combine the chickpeas, parsley, cilantro, scallions, garlic, cumin, harissa, and yogurt and pulse until combined but not completely smooth, about 15 pulses of 2 seconds each. Season with salt to taste.

Use your hands to roll the mixture into 30 walnut-sized balls, keeping a small bowl of water nearby so the dough doesn't stick to your fingers.

To cook, arrange the falafel on a greased baking sheet and roast for 20 minutes, flipping halfway through so they don't burn on the bottom.

These are best eaten right out of the oven.

GRILLED SQUID, WHITE BEAN, AND FENNEL SALAD

Gluten-free, Under 30 minutes
SERVES 4

White bean, fennel, and arugula salad is one of my favorite lunches. Sometimes I add *bo-querones* (Spanish white anchovies) or good canned tuna, but for this variation, we opted for charred calamari and a fresh basil oil. It's really good. —TB

1 pound calamari, cleaned, rinsed, and dried

4 tablespoons olive oil

Zest and juice of 1 lemon

Salt and freshly ground black pepper

¼ to ½ teaspoon chili flakes (or to taste)

A large handful of arugula

2 small or 1 large fennel bulb, cleaned and thinly sliced

1 (15-ounce) can cannellini beans, drained and rinsed

1 medium shallot, thinly sliced

¼ cup chopped fresh parsley

A large pinch of coarse sea salt

Basil Oil (page 242), to taste

Slice the calamari into ½-inch rings and toss with 1 tablespoon of the olive oil, half the lemon zest, a pinch of salt, a few grinds of pepper, and half of the chili flakes.

Divide the arugula among four plates (or place all on a large platter). In a large bowl, combine the fennel, cannellini beans, shallot, parsley, the remaining lemon zest, lemon juice, coarse salt, the remaining chili flakes, and the remaining 3 tablespoons olive oil and toss to combine.

Heat a grill pan over high heat; grill the squid until just charred and crispy, about 5 minutes.

Arrange the fennel–white bean mixture on top of the arugula and top with the grilled squid. Garnish with basil oil.

POACHED ASIAN CHICKEN SALAD

Gluten-free

SERVES 4

While poaching may seem a little old-fashioned, it still happens to be one of my favorite ways to cook chicken. Loading the cooking liquid with aromatics packs an enormous flavor punch, and the meat is always moist. Serve this as a light dinner with a glass of crisp Riesling.

FOR THE CHICKEN

2 bone-in chicken breasts

2 large garlic cloves, smashed

1 teaspoon salt

1 (1-inch) piece fresh ginger, cut into ¼-inch slices

OR

2 cups shredded cooked chicken

FOR THE DRESSING

2 tablespoons diced shallot (about 1 small shallot)

2 tablespoons champagne vinegar

2 tablespoons lime juice (from about 1 juicy lime)

2 tablespoons tamari

1 teaspoon agave nectar

2 teaspoons hazelnut oil

¼ cup olive oil

Salt and freshly ground black pepper

FOR THE SALAD

2 large zucchini, cut in half lengthwise

24 asparagus spears, tough ends removed

Salt and freshly ground black pepper, to taste

2 tablespoons olive oil

1 head butter lettuce, washed and torn into large pieces

A large handful of fresh mint leaves, roughly chopped

A large handful of fresh cilantro leaves, roughly chopped

2 medium carrots, peeled and grated

To cook the chicken, place all the chicken ingredients in a small saucepan (just large enough to hold the chicken breasts) and add water to cover by 1 inch. Bring the water to a boil, cover, and reduce the heat to the lowest setting; simmer gently for 10 minutes. Turn off the heat and let the chicken sit in the hot liquid for 3 minutes more. When firm and completely cooked, transfer the chicken to a plate to cool; remove and discard the skin and bones and shred the meat into small pieces.

Meanwhile, to make the dressing, whisk together the first 7 ingredients in a small bowl and season to taste with salt and pepper.

To make the salad, heat a grill pan over high heat. Toss the zucchini and asparagus with the olive oil, season with salt and pepper, and grill until charred on one side, then flip and cook until both sides have grill marks, about 5 minutes total. Remove from the grill pan and cut into bite-sized pieces.

Toss the lettuce with the herbs, carrots, and half the dressing and divide among four plates or transfer to a serving platter.

Toss the chicken, asparagus, and zucchini with the remaining dressing and arrange them on top of the lettuce.

QUICK SUMMER PASTAS, TWO WAYS

Pasta is a perfect meal; quick prep time, always comforting. In the next two recipes, a simple combination of garlic, lemon, and fresh herbs makes a surprisingly complex sauce for linguine. We've included two variations here: one with cherry tomatoes and one with grilled Santa Barbara spot prawns.

LEMON AND HERB PASTA WITH CHERRY TOMATOES

Vegetarian, Under 30 minutes

SERVES 4

Make this simple pasta dish in the summertime when cherry tomatoes are sweet and inexpensive.

Salt

2 tablespoons olive oil

3 large garlic cloves, thinly sliced

A pinch of chili flakes

Finely grated zest of 1 lemon

¾ pound linguine

2 pints cherry tomatoes, cut in half

3 tablespoons chopped fresh parsley leaves

¼ cup chopped fresh basil leaves

3 tablespoons chopped fresh chives

Freshly ground black pepper

About ¾ cup grated Parmesan or ricotta salata cheese

Bring a large pot of heavily salted water to a boil.

Meanwhile, in a very large sauté pan, heat the oil, garlic, chili flakes, and half the lemon zest over medium heat. As soon as the garlic begins to sizzle and smell fragrant, turn off the heat and let the oil infuse.

Add the pasta to the boiling water and cook according to the package instructions until al dente. Reserve 1 cup of the pasta cooking water; drain the pasta and add it to the pan with the garlic oil. Turn the heat to low, add the cherry tomatoes, the remaining lemon zest, the fresh herbs, and a few tablespoons of the pasta water. Toss everything together, adding more pasta water a bit at a time, until you achieve a thin sauce that just coats the linguine.

Season with salt and pepper to taste and serve with lots of grated Parmesan or ricotta salata.

SPOT PRAWN PASTA

Under 30 minutes
SERVES 4 TO 6

Spot prawns are one of the best things about living in California. Similar to a langoustine, they are a seasonal treat found in the Pacific Ocean off the coast of Santa Barbara. The somewhat cruel act of butterflying them live is one I usually reserve for the fish guy (or girl). If you can't find spot prawns, use 1½ pounds peeled and deveined jumbo shrimp instead.

Salt

2 tablespoons olive oil, plus extra as needed

3 garlic cloves, thinly sliced

A pinch of chili flakes

Finely grated zest of 1 lemon

¾ pound linguine

2 tablespoons unsalted butter

8 live spot prawns, or 1½ pounds deveined jumbo shrimp, butterflied

Freshly ground black pepper

2 tablespoons finely chopped fresh parsley

2 tablespoons finely chopped fresh basil

2 tablespoons finely chopped fresh chives

Lemon wedges, for serving

Bring a large pot of heavily salted water to a boil.

Meanwhile, in a very large sauté pan, heat the oil, garlic, chili flakes, and half the lemon zest over medium heat. As soon as the garlic begins to sizzle and smell fragrant, turn off the heat and let the oil infuse.

Add the pasta to the boiling water and cook according to the package instructions until al dente. Reserve 1 cup of the pasta cooking water; drain the pasta and add it to the pan with the garlic oil. Turn the heat to low, add the remaining lemon zest, butter, and 2 to 4 tablespoons of the pasta water. Toss to combine, turn off the heat, and keep warm while you grill the spot prawns.

Heat a grill pan over high heat. Drizzle the spot prawns with olive oil and season generously with salt and pepper. Grill, flesh side down, until browned and cooked through, 3 to 5 minutes.

Toss the pasta with the herbs, plate, and top with the grilled prawns. Serve with lemon wedges on the side.

SALMON SKEWERS WITH CHERMOULA

Gluten-free, Under 30 minutes
SERVES 4

Chermoula is a wonderfully complex North African sauce made with toasted cumin seeds, fresh parsley and cilantro, and lots of lemon and garlic. Delicious poured over any grilled meat, fish, or veggies, I find it complements salmon particularly well. In this recipe, it does double-duty as both marinade and sauce. Ask for a center-cut piece of salmon—you want the whole piece to be about 1 inch thick.

2 pounds salmon, skin and bones removed

1 teaspoon cumin seeds, quickly toasted in a dry sauté pan until fragrant

1 cup roughly chopped fresh parsley leaves

1 cup roughly chopped fresh cilantro leaves

1 garlic clove, very finely minced

Zest and juice of ½ lemon

A pinch of chili flakes

A pinch of salt

⅓ cup olive oil

3 tablespoons whole milk yogurt

Soak 8 wooden skewers in water for 20 minutes.

Cut the salmon into generous 1-inch pieces and place in a bowl or baking dish.

To make the chermoula, in a blender, combine all the remaining ingredients except the yogurt and blend for 1 minute, or until smooth. Pour half the chermoula over the salmon, add a generous pinch of salt, and mix well. Allow the mixture to marinate for at least 10 minutes or up to overnight in the fridge.

Combine the remaining chermoula with the yogurt and store in the fridge until ready to serve.

When ready to cook, divide the salmon pieces evenly among the skewers and heat a grill or grill pan over medium-high heat. Grill the salmon for 5 minutes on each side, or until the pieces are all nicely browned and cooked through.

Serve the skewers with the chermoula-yogurt sauce.

SOFT POLENTA WITH ROASTED CHERRY TOMATOES

Vegetarian, Gluten-free, Under 30 minutes
SERVES 4

Creamy polenta and sweet blistered cherry tomatoes make an irresistible combination; add some good-quality burrata to the mix and you'd be a fool to say no. This goes incredibly well with simply grilled meat and a green salad, but it is substantial and satisfying enough to be dinner on its own. The sugar in the cherry tomatoes makes them super sweet and caramelized when roasted—great for flavor, less great for cleanup, so line the baking sheet with parchment paper or aluminum foil to cut down on scrub time.

FOR THE TOMATOES

4 pints cherry tomatoes

1 tablespoon olive oil

Salt and freshly ground black pepper

1 large garlic clove, very finely grated or minced

6 large fresh basil leaves, thinly sliced

FOR THE POLENTA

1 teaspoon salt

1 cup instant polenta

⅓ cup grated Parmesan cheese

2 tablespoons unsalted butter

8 ounces burrata or mozzarella cheese, for serving

To make the tomatoes, preheat the oven to 450°F. Arrange the cherry tomatoes in an even layer on a large baking sheet. Toss with the olive oil and a couple of generous pinches of salt and pepper. Roast for 10 minutes, or until burnished and starting to pop. Remove from the oven and toss with the garlic and basil.

Meanwhile, make the polenta. In a medium saucepan, bring 3 cups water plus the salt to a boil. Add the polenta and cook according to the package instructions. Add the Parmesan and butter and transfer to a serving platter or bowl. Top with the roasted tomatoes and torn burrata cheese.

SPRING FATTOUSH SALAD

Vegetarian, Under 30 minutes
SERVES 4

Fattoush is a popular Middle Eastern salad made up of assorted lettuces and vegetables, some sort of toasted flatbread, and tons of fresh herbs. Add grilled chicken or fish to make this a main course or pair with grilled Salmon Skewers with Chermoula (page 148). You may need to add more lemon juice, olive oil, and sumac to get the right consistency and balance of flavors.

FOR THE DRESSING

1 large garlic clove, very finely grated or minced

Juice of 1 large lemon

¼ cup olive oil

Salt

FOR THE SALAD

2 tablespoons olive oil

1 piece naan bread, torn into roughly ½-inch pieces

2 cups snap peas, cut into ½-inch slices on a bias

1 cup cherry tomatoes, cut in half

1 cup chopped English cucumber (about ½ English cucumber)

4 radishes, thinly sliced

A large handful of arugula

1½ cups finely chopped romaine

½ cup roughly chopped fresh mint

½ cup roughly chopped fresh cilantro

2 scallions, thinly sliced

A large pinch of sumac

4 ounces crumbled feta (optional)

To make the dressing, whisk together the first three ingredients and season with salt to taste. Set aside.

To make the salad, in a medium sauté pan, heat the olive oil over high heat. Toast the naan bread in the pan until lightly browned. Set aside to cool.

Combine the toasted naan and remaining salad ingredients in a large bowl; add the dressing and toss to combine.

SZECHUAN-STYLE GREEN BEANS

Vegan, Gluten-free, Under 30 minutes
SERVES 4

When I was in college in NYC, my sister and I would often meet for lunch dates at Joe's Shanghai in Chinatown. They're famous for their soup dumplings (which we always got at least two orders of), but I love their Szechuan-style string beans, pan-fried to perfection in a spicy soy-based sauce with ground pork, almost as much. These are my pork-free homage. Be careful, they're spicy. —TB

Salt

2 teaspoons minced fresh ginger

2 teaspoons sambal oelek

1 tablespoon tamari

1 teaspoon toasted sesame oil

1 teaspoon maple syrup

½ pound green beans

3 tablespoons olive or peanut oil

Toasted sesame seeds, for garnish (optional)

Bring a large pot of salted water to a boil for the green beans.

In a small bowl, combine the ginger, sambal oelek, tamari, sesame oil, and maple syrup to make the sauce.

Add the green beans to the boiling water and cook just until the water comes back to a boil, about 3 minutes; drain well and dry on a kitchen towel.

Heat the olive oil in a large sauté pan or wok over high heat. When the oil is very hot but not smoking, add the green beans and cook until sizzling and beginning to blister, about 3 minutes. Add the sauce, turn off the heat, and let sit for 2 minutes before serving. Garnish with sesame seeds, if desired.

THAI-STYLE CRAB CAKES

SERVES 4

I LOVE crab cakes in any form, but these, packed with Southeast Asian flavors and tons of fresh herbs, are my new favorite. Don't skip the lemongrass mayo—it really brings this dish together.

FOR THE CAKES

1 pound cooked crabmeat, large pieces broken up a bit

1 tablespoon finely chopped fresh Thai basil or regular basil

1 tablespoon finely chopped fresh cilantro

3 tablespoons Vegenaise

3 scallions, thinly sliced

1 large egg

1 tablespoon fish sauce

½ teaspoon sriracha or other hot sauce

½ teaspoon very finely grated or minced lime zest

½ cup panko bread crumbs

¼ teaspoon kosher salt

FOR THE SAUCE

½ cup Vegenaise

1 medium stalk fresh lemongrass, tough outer layers removed, tender inner portion sliced (about 3 tablespoons)

1 teaspoon very finely grated or minced lime zest

1 tablespoon fresh lime juice

Salt, to taste

Olive oil

To make the crab cakes, in a large bowl, combine all the crab cake ingredients and mix well with your hands. Cover with plastic wrap and let firm up in the fridge for at least 20 minutes or up to 24 hours.

Meanwhile, to make the sauce, in a food processor or high-speed blender, combine all the sauce ingredients and blend until mostly smooth.

When ready to eat, form the crab cake mixture into 8 equal patties, compacting them a bit so they stick together. Heat 2 tablespoons or so of olive oil in a large nonstick sauté pan and cook the crab cakes until crispy on both sides, about 5 minutes total. Serve with the sauce on the side.

TIKKA MASALA ROAST CHICKEN

Gluten-free
SERVES 4

For this fun twist on a classic, a simple roast chicken is amped up with the complex flavors of Indian chicken tikka masala. The yogurt helps keep the chicken moist, and the natural sugar in the tomato paste creates a beautifully burnished, crispy skin. Serve with Indian Creamed Spinach (page 103) and Roasted Cauliflower with Curry and Lime (page 117).

2 garlic cloves, very finely grated or minced

1 thumb-sized piece fresh ginger, peeled and very finely grated or minced

1 tablespoon tomato paste

¼ cup whole milk yogurt

1 teaspoon garam masala

1 teaspoon tandoori spice

1½ teaspoons salt

2 tablespoons olive oil

1 whole chicken (roughly 3½ to 4 pounds), spatchcocked or butterflied

Preheat the oven to 400°F.

In a medium bowl, whisk together the garlic, ginger, tomato paste, yogurt, garam masala, tandoori spice, salt, and olive oil.

Rub the marinade all over the chicken, making sure to get as much as possible underneath the skin.

Place the chicken on a wire rack positioned over an aluminum foil–lined baking sheet (or in a roasting pan or baking dish) and roast for 1 hour and 15 minutes. Check after 40 minutes, and if the chicken is browning too much, cover with foil.

Let rest for at least 10 minutes before carving.

EGGPLANT AND GROUND TURKEY STIR-FRY

Gluten-free
SERVES 4

This will look like an absurd amount of eggplant, but it cooks down significantly. Depending on the size of your wok or pan, you may have to cook it in two batches.

6 tablespoons peanut or safflower oil

2 medium eggplant, peeled and cut into ½-inch cubes

½ pound ground turkey

6 garlic cloves, minced

1 (2-inch) piece fresh ginger, peeled and minced

1 to 2 red jalapeños, seeded, deveined, and finely minced

4 teaspoons tamari

5 tablespoons fish sauce

Juice of 1 lime

4 teaspoons agave

1 tablespoon sriracha

4 scallions, thinly sliced

½ cup chopped fresh basil leaves

¼ cup chopped fresh cilantro

Heat 4 tablespoons of the oil in a wok or large sauté pan over high heat. Add the eggplant and cook, stirring frequently, until browned. Reduce the heat to medium-low, cover, and steam until tender, about 5 minutes.

Move the eggplant to one side of the wok (or remove from the sauté pan to make room), and raise the heat to high. Add the remaining 2 tablespoons oil, the turkey, garlic, ginger, and jalapeños and cook, breaking up the turkey with a wooden spoon, until browned and cooked through, 5 to 7 minutes.

Meanwhile, in a small bowl, whisk together the tamari, fish sauce, lime juice, agave, and sriracha.

Add the sauce (and the eggplant if you removed it), scallions, and three-quarters of the herbs to the wok and turn off the heat. Taste for seasoning and garnish with the remaining herbs.

ZUCCHINI "NOODLES" WITH SPINACH PESTO

Vegetarian, Gluten-free, Under 30 minutes
SERVES 4

I was shocked when my kids destroyed a whole plate of this veggie-packed pesto "pasta"; apparently everyone loves zoodles! Zucchini noodles release a lot of natural liquid as they sit, so try to eat these soon after you toss them with the sauce. Any leftover pesto will keep in the fridge for a couple of weeks and is wonderful spread on sandwiches, stirred into soups, or tossed with cooked veggies.

1 large bunch of fresh basil, chopped (about ½ cup packed)

A large handful of baby spinach (about ½ cup packed)

¼ cup chopped walnuts

1 small garlic clove, finely chopped

Zest of 1 large lemon (about 2 teaspoons)

½ cup olive oil

Salt

½ cup grated Parmesan cheese

Freshly ground black pepper

4 medium zucchini, spiralized

To make the pesto, combine the basil, spinach, walnuts, garlic, lemon zest, olive oil, and a large pinch of salt in a blender or food processor. Blend for 30 seconds to 1 minute, until the mixture is almost completely smooth. Add the Parmesan and season to taste with salt and pepper.

Toss half the pesto with the zucchini noodles, adding more pesto as needed until the noodles are well coated.

ZUCCHINI AND LEEK SOUP

Vegan, Gluten-free, Under 30 minutes
SERVES 4

If you have a Vitamix, this makes the creamiest, most delicious vegan soup imaginable. Seriously, it's hard to believe that it's made up of just seven ingredients, one of which is water. If only all spa food tasted like this! Garnish with torn squash blossoms or very thinly sliced zucchini for a little texture.

¼ cup olive oil

2 large or 4 small leeks, white and light green parts only, cleaned and thinly sliced

3 large garlic cloves, thinly sliced

4 medium zucchini, cut in half lengthwise and sliced into ⅛-inch half-moons

1½ teaspoons salt, or to taste

A pinch of chili flakes

In a heavy-bottomed saucepan or Dutch oven, heat the olive oil and leeks over medium heat and sauté, stirring occasionally, for 10 minutes, or until soft. Add the garlic, zucchini, salt, and chili flakes, cover the pan, and steam over medium-low heat for 10 minutes, or until the zucchini is just tender. Transfer the mixture to a high-powered blender with 2 cups water and blend until very smooth. Taste for seasoning and serve hot or cold.

UNEXPECTED GUESTS

Growing up, my parents' home was a hub. Maybe it was because they were artistic and warm, or maybe we just had the best snacks in the neighborhood—whatever the reason, the house was always full of interesting people and what felt like a million kids. These days, my house is a hub in its own right, and while it can be a little hectic at times, I absolutely love the energy and life of having old friends visiting and kids running around. That being said, I never know who's sleeping over, who's popping by, or who's staying for dinner, which can be a little stressful. After a couple of failed attempts at elaborate last-minute dinners for unexpected guests, I developed, and learned to rely on, a handful of recipes perfect for such occasions. This chapter is full of old and new dishes I know I can make quickly and easily (and scale to any party size) while still exciting my dinner guests.

BAGNA CAUDA SALAD

Gluten-free, Under 30 minutes
SERVES 4

Anyone who knows me well knows I'm mad for anchovies. Those salty little umami-packed morsels are one ingredient I could not live without, which makes me a huge fan of pretty much any dish that prominently features them. Bagna cauda, the warm butter, garlic, and anchovy dip that originates from the Piedmont region of Italy, is one of my favorites. Here, instead of dipping crudités into a bowl of bagna cauda, we use the rich, salty, garlicky sauce as a dressing, pouring it over thinly shaved veggies. This makes a stunning first course, but add a soft-boiled egg or two, and you've got yourself a satisfying dinner.

FOR THE SALAD

1 small endive

6 large cauliflower florets

2 medium carrots, peeled

2 medium beets

4 radishes

10 Brussels sprouts

1 small head of radicchio, cut into 1-inch ribbons

FOR THE DRESSING

6 anchovies

4 tablespoons (½ cup) unsalted butter

¼ cup plus 2 tablespoons olive oil

2 garlic cloves, very finely grated or minced

Zest and juice of 1 lemon

3 tablespoons red wine vinegar

Salt and freshly ground black pepper

To make the salad, separate the endive leaves, use a mandoline to thinly slice the cauliflower florets, carrots, beets, and radishes, and separate the Brussels sprouts into individual leaves. Arrange these and the radicchio on four plates or one platter.

To make the dressing, combine the anchovies, butter, olive oil, and garlic in a small saucepan over medium-low heat. Cook until the anchovies have melted into the sauce and the garlic smells fragrant, 3 to 5 minutes. Add the lemon zest and juice and the vinegar, and season to taste with salt and pepper. Pour over the vegetables and serve immediately.

BRUSSELS SPROUTS AND RAPINI SALAD

Under 30 minutes

SERVES 4

I'm mildly obsessed with rapini (commonly referred to as broccoli rabe), and include it in as many dishes as possible. One day, as I was cleaning some for the Rapini Pasta recipe (page 116), I started munching on the raw leaves and tender florets and realized they would be delicious in a salad. I tossed them in a bowl with shaved Brussels sprouts, a punchy Caesar-inspired dressing, crispy bread crumbs, and lots of grated Parmesan cheese, and my new favorite salad was born. Try to assemble the salad 10 minutes before serving so that the Brussels sprouts and rapini have a chance to soak up all the lovely flavors of the dressing. We love serving this alongside Chicken Piccata (page 138) or Cauliflower Mac 'n' Cheese (page 95). —TB

FOR THE DRESSING

4 anchovies

Juice of 1 large lemon

1 garlic clove, minced

1 tablespoon Vegenaise

1 tablespoon Dijon mustard

6 tablespoons olive oil

Salt and freshly ground black pepper

FOR THE SALAD

1 pound Brussels sprouts, ends and dirty outer leaves removed

4 large handfuls of rapini (broccoli rabe), chopped

2 tablespoons olive oil

⅓ cup bread crumbs

Salt and freshly ground black pepper

Zest of 1 lemon

Grated Parmesan cheese, for garnish

To make the dressing, blend the first 6 dressing ingredients together in a high-powered blender, then season with salt and pepper.

To make the salad, use the slicing blade of a food processor or a mandoline to shave the Brussels sprouts into thin slices and toss them in a large bowl. Tear or slice large rapini leaves into bite-sized pieces and cut any large florets in half; add to the bowl with the Brussels sprouts.

Heat the olive oil in a small sauté pan. Add the bread crumbs and toast until lightly browned; season with salt and pepper and stir in the lemon zest.

Add the lemony bread crumbs to the bowl with the rapini and sprouts, toss with the dressing, and finish with finely grated Parmesan cheese.

CRISPY POTATOES
WITH LEMON AND PARSLEY

Vegan, Gluten-free, Under 30 minutes
SERVES 4

Boiling new potatoes in heavily salted water gets them seasoned and tender quickly, before being tossed in hot oil for a crispy golden crust. The smaller your potatoes are, the faster they'll cook, so be sure to check for doneness with a sharp knife every so often as they boil. These are really good with Three-Mustard Chicken (page 191) or Turkey Meat Loaf (page 124).

2 pounds new potatoes or fingerlings

Lots of coarse sea salt

¼ cup olive oil

Zest of 1 lemon, very finely grated

1 large garlic clove, very finely minced

¼ cup chopped fresh parsley

Put the potatoes in a large saucepan and add water to cover and a very generous pinch of salt. Bring the water to a boil, reduce the heat, and simmer until the potatoes are just cooked through, about 15 minutes, depending on size.

Drain the potatoes, allow them to cool slightly, then use your hands or the side of a knife to softly crush each one.

Meanwhile, heat the olive oil in a large sauté pan over medium-high heat; when the oil is very hot but not smoking, add the potatoes and let sit, undisturbed, until brown and crispy on one side. Use a large spatula to turn the potatoes over, allowing the other side to crisp up, too. Add the lemon zest, garlic, and parsley, stir, and cook for another minute. Season generously with coarse sea salt and serve.

CAULIFLOWER AND KIMCHI "FRIED RICE"

Vegan, Gluten-free, Under 30 minutes
SERVES 4

I once stopped for lunch in Oakland because the sign out front read "I bleed Kimchi." Yeah, me too. This "fried rice" is seriously good. Plus, it's grain-free, vegan, and full of probiotic-packed kimchi, which means it's really good for you, too. Serve with Szechuan-Style Green Beans (page 159) or Shrimp Stir-Fry (page 84).

1 small head of cauliflower	2 scallions, thinly sliced
2 tablespoons safflower oil	½ cup chopped kimchi
2 teaspoons toasted sesame oil	¼ cup chopped fresh cilantro
1 small bunch of dinosaur (lacinato) kale, ribs removed, leaves sliced into ribbons	3 tablespoons tamari

Cut the cauliflower into small florets, then pulse in a food processor until the pieces are the size of couscous (you should have about 2 cups).

Heat the safflower and sesame oils in a large nonstick sauté pan over high heat. Add the kale and cauliflower and sauté until the kale is wilted and the cauliflower is beginning to brown, 3 to 5 minutes. Mix in the scallions, kimchi, cilantro, and tamari. Taste for seasoning and serve.

FISH IN PARCHMENT, THREE WAYS

Cooking fish in little parchment parcels (called *en papillote* in French) is a very old-school French technique; it also happens to be one of my favorite ways to cook fish for a crowd. It stays super moist, the cleanup is easy, and the presentation is always impressive. Folding up the parchment does take a bit of practice, though, so make these recipes for close friends or family a couple of times until you've got the technique down. Here are three of our favorite flavor combos, but feel free to play around with any mix of seafood and ingredients. These recipes all make four individual servings, but it's also fun to make one large parcel and let guests serve themselves family-style.

NIÇOISE PETRALE SOLE

Gluten-free, Under 30 Minutes
SERVES 4

4 petrale sole fillets, or whatever white-fleshed fish looks best

Salt and freshly ground black pepper

2 teaspoons capers

12 cherry tomatoes, cut in half

16 pitted kalamata olives, cut in half

4 teaspoons white wine

4 teaspoons olive oil

4 teaspoons julienned fresh basil

Preheat the oven to 400ºF.

Lay out four 9 × 11-inch pieces of parchment paper on a flat surface. Season the sole fillets generously with salt and pepper and place one in the lower third section of each parchment sheet. Top each with ½ teaspoon capers, 3 sliced cherry tomatoes, and 4 halved kalamata olives. Carefully pour 1 teaspoon white wine and 1 teaspoon olive oil over each, then fold the top half of the parchment paper over the fish to make a rectangle. Starting with one edge, tightly roll up the parchment paper until no liquid can escape. Repeat with the other two edges, then place the parcels on a baking sheet and bake for 10 to 15 minutes, depending on the thickness of the fillets.

Transfer the parcels to a plate and allow guests to tear open the packages and garnish their portions with julienned basil.

MIXED SEAFOOD
WITH SHERRY AND SAFFRON

Gluten-free, Under 30 minutes
SERVES 4

1 medium shallot, thinly sliced

16 small clams, such as manila or littleneck

12 medium shrimp

16 bay scallops, or 8 diver scallops

1 large garlic clove, thinly sliced

2 tablespoons unsalted butter

4 teaspoons sherry

4 small pinches of saffron threads

4 teaspoons finely chopped fresh parsley

Fresh lemon juice, to finish

Preheat the oven to 400°F.

Lay out four 9 × 11-inch pieces of parchment paper on a flat surface and divide the sliced shallot evenly among them; top each pile with 4 clams, 3 shrimp, and 4 bay scallops. Divide the garlic among the four sheets, then add ½ tablespoon butter, 1 teaspoon sherry, and 1 small pinch of saffron to each. Carefully fold the top half of the parchment paper over the fish to make a rectangle, then, starting with one edge, tightly roll up the parchment paper until no liquid can escape. Repeat with the other two edges, then place the parcels on a baking sheet and bake for about 10 minutes, until all the seafood is cooked through and the clams have opened.

Transfer the parcels to a plate and allow guests to tear open the packages and garnish their portions with fresh chopped parsley and fresh lemon juice.

ASIAN-STEAMED HALIBUT
WITH SCALLIONS AND BOK CHOY

Gluten-free, Under 30 minutes
SERVES 4

4 scallions, sliced

4 baby bok choy, cut in half

1 thumb-sized piece fresh ginger, peeled and thinly sliced

4 (5- to 6-ounce) halibut fillets, bones and skin removed

Salt and freshly ground black pepper

4 teaspoons toasted sesame oil

4 teaspoons mirin

4 teaspoons tamari

Preheat the oven to 400°F.

Lay out four 9 × 11-inch pieces of parchment paper on a flat surface, and place one-quarter of the sliced scallions, 1 bok choy, and one-eighth of the sliced ginger in the lower third section of each piece. Place 1 halibut fillet on each bed of veggies and season the fish with salt and pepper. Arrange the remaining sliced ginger on top of the fish and pour 1 teaspoon each of the sesame oil, mirin, and tamari over each fillet. Carefully fold the top half of the parchment paper over the fish to make a rectangle; then, starting with one edge, tightly roll up the parchment paper until no liquid can escape. Repeat with the other two edges, then place the parcels on a baking sheet and bake for 15 to 20 minutes, depending on how thick your fillets are.

Transfer the parcels to plates so diners can tear open the packages.

GRILLED ROMAINE AND SHRIMP "COBB" SALAD

Gluten-free, Under 30 minutes
SERVES 4

There is a lot going on in this salad, but trust me, the seemingly disparate flavors come together to create something out-of-this-world delicious. Be sure to get your grill pan nice and hot before you add the lettuce; you want it to sear while still retaining some crunch.

FOR THE DRESSING

2 teaspoons Dijon mustard

¼ cup finely minced shallot

2 tablespoons Vegenaise

2 tablespoons red wine vinegar

6 tablespoons olive oil

½ cup crumbled blue cheese

Salt and freshly ground black pepper

FOR THE SALAD

8 slices thick bacon, cut into ½-inch pieces

Four 9-minute eggs (page 244), whites and yolks separated

4 heads baby romaine, cut in half, rinsed, and dried well

Salt and freshly ground black pepper

16 large shrimp, peeled and deveined

1 tablespoon olive oil

24 cherry tomatoes, cut in half

1 large or 2 small avocados, pitted, peeled, and diced

¼ cup finely chopped fresh chives

To make the dressing, whisk together the mustard, shallot, Vegenaise, and vinegar; slowly drizzle in the olive oil, whisking continuously to emulsify. Add the blue cheese and season with salt and pepper to taste.

To make the salad, cook the bacon in a medium sauté pan until crispy; transfer to a paper towel–lined plate, making sure to reserve the fat. While the bacon cooks, cut the egg whites into a small dice and use your fingers to crumble the egg yolks.

Heat a grill pan over medium-high heat. Brush the flat sides of each romaine half with bacon fat and season with salt and pepper. Grill the lettuce, flat side down, for about 5 minutes, or until wilted and nicely charred on one side. Transfer to a plate. You may have to do this in batches, depending on how big your grill pan is.

When all the lettuce is grilled, toss the shrimp in the olive oil, season to taste with salt and pepper, and grill for 2 to 3 minutes on each side, or until pink with nice grill marks.

To assemble the salad, place two halves romaine, grilled side up, on a plate. Top with tomatoes, avocado, shrimp, and egg white.

Spoon over half the dressing, then garnish with crumbled egg yolk, crispy bacon, and chopped chives. Serve with extra dressing on the side.

THREE-MUSTARD CHICKEN

SERVES 4

This sauce, which comprises three kinds of mustard (Dijon, grainy mustard, and wasabi), a little Vegenaise, and a touch of maple syrup to balance the spice, yields the moistest, most flavorful baked chicken ever. Grilling the breasts first gives the dish an added layer of flavor, but if you're low on time, simply slather the raw breasts with the sauce, top with bread crumbs, and add 10 minutes to the baking time. Airline chicken breasts are boneless, skin-on breasts with the little wing bone still attached, but if you can't find them, boneless, skin-on breasts work just fine.

4 airline (or boneless, skin-on) chicken breasts, at room temperature

Salt and freshly ground black pepper

2 tablespoons olive oil

¼ cup Dijon mustard

¼ cup grainy mustard

2 teaspoons wasabi powder

2 tablespoons Vegenaise

1 tablespoon champagne vinegar

2 tablespoons maple syrup

½ cup bread crumbs

Preheat the oven to 350°F.

Season the chicken breasts liberally with salt and pepper and coat in 1 tablespoon of the olive oil; grill over medium heat in a hot grill pan until nicely browned, about 3 minutes per side.

Meanwhile, in a small bowl, combine the remaining 1 tablespoon olive oil, the mustards, wasabi powder, Vegenaise, vinegar, and maple syrup and season to taste with salt and pepper.

When the chicken is nicely browned, transfer it to a baking dish that will hold the breasts snugly. Let cool slightly until cool enough to handle. Use your hands to rub the mustard mixture all over the chicken, being sure to get a lot of sauce under the skin. Top each breast with 2 tablespoons of the bread crumbs, pop the dish in the oven, and bake for 30 minutes, or until the bread crumbs are crispy and brown and the chicken is cooked through.

ASPARAGUS MIMOSA

Vegetarian, Gluten-free, Under 30 minutes
SERVES 4 TO 6

Named after the yellow-and-white mimosa flower, the beautiful (and awesomely retro) hard-boiled egg garnish really makes this dish. Serve this in the spring when asparagus is in season.

FOR THE DRESSING

2 teaspoons Dijon mustard

1 teaspoon grainy mustard

2 tablespoons red wine vinegar

1½ tablespoons finely minced shallot

3 tablespoons olive oil

Salt and freshly ground black pepper

FOR THE ASPARAGUS

2 bunches of asparagus, tough ends removed

3 tablespoons olive oil

Salt and freshly ground black pepper

Two 11-minute eggs (page 244), whites and yolks separated

Coarse sea salt, for serving

To make the dressing, in a small bowl, whisk together the Dijon mustard, grainy mustard, vinegar, shallot, and olive oil. Season to taste with salt and pepper.

To make the asparagus, heat a grill pan over medium-high heat. Toss the asparagus with the olive oil, salt, and pepper and grill until nicely charred and just tender, about 5 minutes.

While the asparagus cooks, cut the egg whites into very small dice and crumble the egg yolks with your fingers.

To assemble, place the asparagus on individual plates or a large platter, drizzle over the mustard dressing, and top with the chopped boiled egg. Finish with a pinch of coarse sea salt and freshly ground pepper.

ROASTED BEET AND BLUE CHEESE SALAD

Vegetarian, Gluten-free
SERVES 4

Much to my children's chagrin, our house is always stocked with an impressive assortment of stinky cheeses, at least one of which is blue. I'd eat blue cheese on almost anything, but its tangy flavor is particularly well balanced by the earthy sweetness of roasted beets and slightly bitter radicchio and endive in this salad. Use red beets if you can't find golden, but be warned: their gorgeous magenta hue will dye the entire salad a shocking shade of pink.

FOR THE DRESSING

2 tablespoons finely diced shallot

3 tablespoons champagne vinegar

2 teaspoons balsamic vinegar

1 tablespoon hazelnut oil

¼ cup olive oil

Salt and freshly ground black pepper

FOR THE SALAD

4 ounces crumbled blue cheese, such as Roquefort

8 small golden beets, cooked, peeled, and cut into roughly ½-inch pieces*

4 handfuls of thinly sliced radicchio (from about ½ medium head)

2 endives, thinly sliced

2 tablespoons finely diced shallot

Four 9-minute eggs (page 244), peeled and cut into roughly ½-inch pieces

To make the dressing, whisk together the first 5 dressing ingredients and season to taste with salt and pepper.

To make the salad, combine all the salad ingredients in a large bowl and toss with half the dressing. Taste for seasoning, transfer to plates or a large platter, and serve with the remaining dressing on the side.

* I think roasted beets taste best; wrap them in aluminum foil with salt, pepper, a little olive oil, and a splash of vinegar, place on a baking sheet, and roast in a preheated 400°F oven for 1 hour. However, if you're short on time, you can also boil them in lightly salted water until tender, or you can buy them cooked at many grocery stores, which makes this salad a breeze to throw together.

SEARED SCALLOPS WITH
WATERCRESS AND ASPARAGUS

Gluten-free, Under 30 minutes
SERVES 4

We know scallops intimidate a lot of cooks, but they're actually one of the easiest and quickest types of seafood to prepare. The most important things to remember are to get the skillet nice and hot, to make sure the scallops are dry so they sear rather than steam, and to not touch them until they've developed a nice crust on one side and are almost cooked through. Here we pair them with a warm spring salad and a quick brown butter pan sauce—make this for someone you're trying to impress, or quarter the recipe and treat yourself to a restaurant-quality weeknight feast. You deserve it—you made perfectly cooked scallops!

16 diver scallops

Salt and freshly ground black pepper

Juice of 1 small lemon

A splash of champagne vinegar

1 tablespoon finely diced shallot

4 tablespoons olive oil

12 asparagus spears, tough ends removed

1 bunch of watercress, cleaned and dried

A large handful of sugar snap peas, cut into ½-inch slices (about 1 cup)

4 tablespoons (½ stick) unsalted butter

Coarse sea salt

Lemon wedges, for serving (optional)

Remove the scallops from the fridge, use a paper towel to dry them very well, and season generously with salt and pepper.

Mix the lemon juice, vinegar, shallot, and 1 tablespoon of the olive oil in the bottom of a large bowl.

Use a peeler to shave 4 of the asparagus spears and add them to the bowl along with the watercress. Cut the remaining 8 asparagus spears into ½-inch pieces and set aside.

Heat a large sauté pan over medium-high heat. Add 1 tablespoon of the olive oil, the snap peas, and the asparagus pieces, season with salt and pepper, and sauté for 1 to 2 minutes, or until just barely cooked. Add to the bowl with the watercress and shaved asparagus.

Add the remaining 2 tablespoons olive oil to the sauté pan, then add the scallops, leaving them to sear on one side, undisturbed, until very crispy and almost cooked through, 3 to 5 minutes. Flip the scallops, then reduce the heat to low and add the butter. The butter will immediately sizzle and start to turn brown. Turn off the heat (the residual heat will finish cooking the scallops).

Toss the watercress-asparagus salad to combine well. Divide the salad among four plates (or arrange it on one platter), arrange the cooked scallops on top of the salad, and pour the brown butter over. Garnish with a little coarse sea salt and serve with lemon wedges on the side, if desired.

SHISHITO PEPPERS

Vegan, Gluten-free, Under 30 minutes
SERVES 4

Shishitos are one of my favorite sides—I've had them stuffed, deep-fried in tempura batter, and dusted with dried fish roe called bottarga (all of which were delicious, by the way), but my preferred preparation is still the simplest: sautéed in a hot pan with oil until blistered and beginning to soften, then sprinkled with a hit of really good coarse sea salt. Much like padrón peppers, about 1 in 10 are spicy, so get ready to play pepper roulette.

Olive oil

¾ **pound shishito peppers**

Coarse sea salt

Cheat's Aioli (page 248)

Heat a wok or large sauté pan over high heat. Add a glug of olive oil and when it is hot but not yet smoking, add the peppers. Cook, stirring often, until the peppers are blistered and just softened, 5 to 10 minutes (cover with a lid for a few minutes if the peppers are not softening quickly enough). Season generously with sea salt and serve with the aioli, for dipping.

SINGAPORE RICE NOODLES

Vegetarian, Gluten-free, Under 30 minutes
SERVES 4

These pan-fried noodles are gluten free, full of veggies, and kid-approved (my kids inhale this). The prep does take some time, but once you're cooking, the dish comes together quickly, so be ready with all the ingredients. Add chicken, shrimp, or beef for a little extra protein, and if you don't have a wok or a really big nonstick pan, use two smaller pans—these noodles don't like to be crowded. Pan-frying noodles is not an exact science, so trust your instincts and add a couple more glugs of oil if things are looking dry or starting to stick.

3½ ounces thin rice noodles (such as Eden Foods bifun noodles)

4 tablespoons peanut oil

2 tablespoons toasted sesame oil

1 medium yellow onion, thinly sliced

½ cup finely chopped broccoli

½ cup chopped green beans (½-inch pieces)

½ cup fresh or frozen peas

7 ounces firm tofu, cut into ½-inch pieces

1 teaspoon madras curry powder, or more to taste

1 large egg

¼ cup tamari

2 scallions, thinly sliced

¼ cup chopped fresh cilantro

Salt, if desired

Soak the rice noodles in hot water for 10 minutes or according to the package instructions. Meanwhile, heat a wok or large nonstick sauté pan over medium-high heat and add 1 tablespoon each of the peanut and sesame oils. When the oils are hot but not smoking, add the onion and cook, untouched, for 1 minute to sear. Reduce the heat to medium and sauté, stirring occasionally, for 4 minutes more. Transfer the onion to a bowl.

Add the broccoli, green beans, peas, tofu, and another tablespoon of peanut oil to the pan. Sauté over high heat until the veggies are just cooked through and the tofu is beginning to brown (about 2 minutes); transfer the veggies and tofu to the bowl with the onion.

Add 1 tablespoon of the peanut oil, the remaining 1 tablespoon of sesame oil, the soaked and drained noodles, curry powder, and 2 tablespoons water to the pan and stir to combine. Make a hole in the middle of the noodles, add the remaining 1 tablespoon peanut oil, and crack in the egg. Stir vigorously with a wooden spoon and let scramble until almost cooked through, then mix in with the noodles.

Add the tamari, scallions, and cilantro and stir everything to combine. Taste for seasoning, add salt if necessary, and serve.

SOCCA PIZZAS

Vegan, Gluten-free, Under 30 minutes
MAKES 6 "PIZZAS"

I call these "pizzas," because I love to load them up with a bunch of different toppings, but *socca*, made from chickpea flour and little else, are really more like pancakes or thick crepes. Naturally gluten-free and wonderfully versatile, these are delicious topped with any number of ingredients. Here are three of my favorite combos to get you started. Prep all the topping components in advance so you're ready to assemble as the "pizzas" come out of the pan. Kids love to get involved in the assembly process.

2¼ cups chickpea flour	Salt
2 tablespoons olive oil, plus more for frying	Toppings of your choice

To make the batter, whisk together the chickpea flour, olive oil, and 2 cups water and season with 2 big pinches of salt. When ready to cook the pizzas, heat an 8-inch nonstick pan over medium-high heat. Add 2 tablespoons or so of olive oil, pour in about ¼ cup of the batter, and cook for 3 to 5 minutes, until the bottom is crispy and the top is almost set. Carefully flip the socca and cook for 1 minute more. Transfer to a plate and dress with your desired toppings. Repeat with the remaining batter.

PISSALADIÈRE SOCCA

Gluten-free, Under 30 minutes
MAKES 2 SOCCA PIZZAS

Olive oil

1 medium yellow onion, cut in half and thinly sliced

1 teaspoon fresh thyme leaves

1 garlic clove, thinly sliced

2 socca pancakes (page 207)

½ cup cherry tomatoes

1 to 3 anchovies

5 niçoise olives

Cracked black pepper

Heat the olive oil in a medium sauté pan. Add the onion, thyme, and garlic and sauté until the onion is tender and sweet, about 10 minutes. Place the onion directly on the socca, add the cherry tomatoes to the pan, and cook over high heat until beginning to blister. Top the onion with the blistered tomatoes, anchovies, and olives, and season with cracked black pepper.

ZA'ATAR ROASTED CARROT AND AVOCADO

Vegan, Gluten-free, Under 30 minutes
MAKES 2 SOCCA PIZZAS

4 small carrots

Olive oil

Sea salt

Za'atar

2 socca pancakes (page 207)

½ avocado, sliced

2 tablespoons chopped fresh cilantro

Juice of ½ lime

Preheat the oven to 400°F.

On a baking sheet, toss the carrots with about 2 tablespoons of olive oil, a good pinch of salt, and a good pinch of za'atar. Roast for 20 minutes, or until the carrots are nicely browned and tender.

Halve the roasted carrots, arrange them over the socca, then top with sliced avocado and the cilantro. Sprinkle with extra sea salt and za'atar and squeeze fresh lime juice over it all.

BURRATA AND SHAVED VEGGIES

Vegetarian, Gluten-free, Under 30 minutes
MAKES 2 SOCCA PIZZAS

2 or 3 asparagus spears, shaved into ribbons with a peeler

½ small zucchini, shaved into ribbons with a peeler

2 tablespoons chopped fresh mint

Zest and juice of ½ lemon

2 tablespoons olive oil

Sea salt

2 socca pancakes (page 207)

2 ounces burrata cheese

Toss the shaved asparagus, shaved zucchini, mint, lemon zest, lemon juice, olive oil, and a generous pinch of salt together to make a salad. Place directly on the socca and top with the burrata.

ZUNI SHEET PAN CHICKEN

SERVES 4

Zuni Café in San Francisco has an incredible, world-famous roast chicken. It's salted for days, cooked in their gorgeous wood-burning oven, and served over a perfectly balanced bread salad with mustard greens, pine nuts, and currants. This is our weeknight twist with roasted garlic, lemons, and anchovies. The chicken is cut up so it roasts quicker, and everything is cooked in one baking sheet, roasting pan, or large baking dish in an attempt to keep cleanup minimal. Use whatever ovenproof dish you like, just make sure it has sides and is big enough to hold the chicken pieces, torn bread, and lemons. This is dinner party–worthy.

1 whole (3½-pound) chicken, cut into 8 pieces

6 large garlic cloves, unpeeled, smashed with the back of a knife

1 teaspoon very finely chopped fresh rosemary

1 teaspoon very finely chopped fresh thyme

1 teaspoon salt

Freshly ground black pepper

1 lemon, zested with a Microplane then cut in half

4 tablespoons olive oil

½ baguette, torn into roughly 1- to 2-inch pieces

2 anchovies, finely chopped or smashed with a fork

2 tablespoons red wine vinegar

¼ cup water

4 large handfuls of arugula, mustard greens, kale, escarole, or whatever greens you like

Lemon wedges, optional

Preheat the oven to 425°F.

Arrange the chicken pieces skin side up on a large rimmed baking sheet or in a large baking dish or roasting pan and scatter the garlic cloves around them.

In a small bowl, combine the rosemary, thyme, salt, several generous grinds of pepper, the lemon zest, and 1 tablespoon of the olive oil. Mix together and rub all over the chicken, being sure to get some under the skin.

Place the baking sheet in the oven and roast the chicken, undisturbed, for 40 minutes. After 40 minutes, remove from the oven and arrange the torn bread and zested lemon halves in between the chicken pieces, tossing them in any juice the chicken has released. Drizzle everything with another glug of olive oil (about 2 tablespoons) and return the pan to the oven to roast for 10 minutes more.

Meanwhile, combine the anchovies, vinegar, and ¼ cup water in a small bowl and set aside. Place the arugula in a large shallow serving bowl.

Remove the chicken from the oven and immediately add the anchovy mixture—this will help deglaze the pan so you don't lose all those nice crispy bits.

Use tongs (or your fingers) to pluck out the croutons and add them to the serving bowl with the arugula; toss with the remaining 1 tablespoon olive oil and a pinch of salt. Top with the chicken pieces and lightly tent the bowl with aluminum foil.

(Continued)

Next, take the garlic cloves and squeeze them out of their skins back onto the baking sheet and squeeze the roasted lemon halves over the baking sheet to release all their juice.

Use a wooden spoon or spatula to crush the softened garlic cloves and scrape up as much of the crusty bits on the bottom of the pan as possible.

Pour about half the garlicky pan sauce over the chicken and bread salad and serve with the remaining sauce on the side, and lemon wedges to finish, if desired.

SOFT POLENTA WITH
ROASTED ASPARAGUS AND CRISPY PROSCIUTTO

Gluten-free, Under 30 minutes
SERVES 4

I eat no red meat and very little pork, but I must admit I've got a serious soft spot for cured meats like Serrano and Iberico ham and prosciutto. This combo of warm, cheesy polenta, roasted asparagus, crispy prosciutto, and soft-boiled egg is unreal.

24 asparagus spears, tough ends removed	Salt and freshly ground black pepper
1 tablespoon olive oil	8 thin slices prosciutto

FOR THE POLENTA

1 teaspoon salt	1/3 cup grated Parmesan cheese
1 cup instant polenta	2 tablespoons unsalted butter

4 poached or 6-minute eggs (page 244)	Grated Parmesan cheese, for garnish

Preheat the oven to 400°F.

Toss the asparagus with the olive oil, season with salt and pepper, then arrange in an even layer on half a large baking sheet. Spread the prosciutto out on the other half, overlapping the slices slightly if necessary. Roast for 10 minutes, or until the asparagus is tender and the prosciutto is crispy.

Meanwhile, to make the polenta, in a medium saucepan, bring 3 cups water plus the salt to a boil. Add the polenta to the boiling water and cook according to the package instructions, stirring continuously to make sure it doesn't stick. Add the Parmesan and butter and transfer to a serving platter or bowl. Top with the roasted asparagus, crispy prosciutto, eggs, and grated Parmesan.

SOMETHING SWEET

Ice cream, cookies, candy, oh my. Even for my most health-conscious friends, dessert is a temptation that can be hard to resist. And although I don't have much of a sweet tooth myself, I do sometimes like to finish a meal with a little something sweet. While all the savory recipes in this book are healthy, Thea and I did ease up a bit on them, incorporating some dairy or gluten from time to time. But because it's hard to find desserts that aren't full of dairy, fat, and sugar, it was important that all the sweets included be vegan, gluten free, and not contain refined white sugar. Don't judge a vegan dessert book by its cover—all these clean desserts will leave you wanting seconds, with none of the guilt.

BALSAMIC-MACERATED BERRIES
WITH CASHEW CREAM

Vegan, Gluten-free, No refined sugar
SERVES 4

Syrupy balsamic vinegar, usually associated with savory dishes and salads, is actually the perfect complement to sweet summer berries. Toss them together with a pinch of coconut sugar and serve with cashew cream and freshly grated lemon zest; an elegant, foolproof, vegan dessert in minutes. If you don't have time to make cashew cream and can tolerate dairy, this is just as good with whipped cream or lightly sweetened crème fraîche.

2 cups halved strawberries

2 teaspoons thick balsamic vinegar

1 teaspoon coconut sugar

½ to 1 cup Cashew Cream (page 247)

Lemon zest, for garnish

Combine the berries, vinegar, and sugar in a large bowl and gently stir to combine. Divide the berries and cream among four bowls or glasses, and grate a little fresh lemon zest over.

CHOCOLATE BANANA MILK SHAKE

Vegan, Gluten-free, No refined sugar, Under 30 minutes
MAKES 1 LARGE MILK SHAKE

This flavor combo is my son Moses's jam. He loves a milk shake made with Nutella, banana, and vanilla ice cream (and who wouldn't?!), but I worry about all that refined sugar. Because I'm always looking for ways to make the staple recipes in our house a little healthier, I set to work developing a refined sugar-free and dairy-free version that would get his (sometimes hard to come by) stamp of approval. I'm happy to report that, although he's still a die-hard Nutella fan, he'll happily down this for dessert any night of the week.

6 tablespoons oat milk

1 banana, peeled and frozen

1 teaspoon almond butter

1 teaspoon raw cacao powder

¼ cup non-dairy coconut ice cream

Combine all the ingredients in a high-powered blender and blend until smooth.

CHOCOLATE MOUSSE

Vegan, Gluten-free, No refined sugar
SERVES 4

Even the ice cream–eating, milk chocolate–loving men in our lives agree that this super-sneaky healthy recipe is bomb, especially with a dollop of cashew cream and some flaky sea salt to finish. We find that the flavor improves with time, so make it at least 1 hour, and preferably a day, before you want to serve it.

1 large avocado, pitted and peeled

2 tablespoons almond butter

Sea salt

¼ teaspoon vanilla powder or vanilla extract

¼ cup brown rice syrup

¼ cup maple syrup

¼ cup raw cacao or unsweetened Dutch-processed cocoa powder

¼ cup almond milk

¼ teaspoon liquid stevia

2 tablespoons coconut oil

½ to 1 cup Cashew Cream (page 247)

In a blender or food processor, combine the avocado, almond butter, a large pinch of salt, vanilla powder, brown rice syrup, maple syrup, cacao, almond milk, stevia, and coconut oil and blend for 2 minutes, or until very smooth. Divide among four ramekins; cover and refrigerate for at least 1 hour.

Serve topped with a dollop of cashew cream and a pinch of sea salt.

CHOCOLATE TRUFFLES

Vegan, Gluten-free, No refined sugar, Under 30 minutes
MAKES 16 SMALL TRUFFLES

These are so easy to make and dangerously addictive. If you can't find date syrup, use 2 table-spoons of agave nectar instead.

½ cup raw cacao or unsweetened Dutch-processed cocoa powder

2 tablespoons date syrup or agave nectar

2 tablespoons coconut oil, plus more as needed

2 pinches of Maldon or other sea salt

½ teaspoon vanilla extract

6 drops of liquid stevia

6 tablespoons chia seeds

Combine the cacao, date syrup, coconut oil, salt, vanilla, and stevia in a medium bowl and use your hands to work it into a smooth mixture, adding a bit more coconut oil if needed.

Pour the chia seeds into a shallow dish. Form the cacao mixture into 16 balls and roll each one in the chia seeds. Chill in the fridge until ready to eat.

COCONUT KEY LIME TARTS

Vegan, Gluten-free, No refined sugar

MAKES EIGHT 2½-INCH TARTS

Key lime pie is one of my daughter's favorite desserts, so I've made a lot of them over the years. While I'm a big fan of the sweetened condensed milk and sugar bomb that is the traditional recipe, I wanted to make a raw, vegan dessert highlighting the bright, citrusy flavor I love so much in the original without all the butter, sugar, and preservatives. Use natural almond meal or flour if you can find it, and be sure to put your coconut milk in the fridge overnight so the solids and liquids separate.

FOR THE CRUST

1 cup natural almond meal or flour

3 tablespoons coconut oil

3 tablespoons brown rice syrup

A pinch of salt

FOR THE FILLING

1 (13.5-ounce) can full-fat coconut milk, left in the fridge overnight

Zest of 5 key limes or 1 regular lime, plus extra for garnish

Juice of 3 key limes or 1 regular lime

2 tablespoons plus 1 teaspoon coconut sugar

To make the crust, place all the crust ingredients in a medium bowl and use your hands to mix thoroughly, making sure there are no lumps of coconut oil left. Divide the mixture into 8 (about 1 tablespoon each) balls if using a standard muffin tin or 24 (about 1 teaspoon each) balls if using a mini-muffin tin. Place one ball of dough in each well of the muffin tin. Wet your fingers with water and press the dough up the sides to make little tart shells. Place the tart shells in the fridge to set while you make the filling.

To make the filling, scoop out the solid portion of the coconut milk (leaving it in the fridge overnight allows the fat to separate from the liquid) and place it in a large bowl. Use a fork to break it up into an almost smooth consistency, then add the lime zest, lime juice, and coconut sugar. Whisk until the mixture is super smooth and has the consistency of lightly whipped cream. Fill each tart shell with the coconut filling, garnish with extra lime zest, and refrigerate until firm, at least 1 hour.

When ready to eat, use a butter knife to loosen the tarts from the pan, then pop them out. Eat immediately or store in the fridge so they keep their shape.

COCONUT COOKIES

Vegan, Gluten-free, No refined sugar, Under 30 minutes
MAKES 16 COOKIES

If you like coconut, you'll love these. They're chewy and not overly sweet, which makes them perfect for breakfast or tea, as well as dessert. I like strawberry or apricot jam best—just be sure to use a natural one with no refined sugar. I originally made these plain, until my daughter suggested the dollop of jam in the center. Well played, Apple.

¼ cup coconut sugar

¼ cup coconut oil

2 cups unsweetened shredded coconut

½ cup coconut flour

½ cup brown rice syrup

4 teaspoons jam of your choice

Preheat the oven to 350ºF.

Combine all the ingredients except the jam in a large bowl; use your hands or a wooden spoon to form the mixture into a large ball, pressing to compact it. Wet your hands with water, divide the dough into 2 equal balls, then divide each ball into 8 golf ball–sized cookies (to make 16 cookies total). Place the cookies on a baking sheet and use your thumb to make an indentation in the middle of each one. Fill each indentation with about ¼ teaspoon of the jam and bake for 12 to 15 minutes, or until golden.

Let cool before eating.

COCONUT PUDDINGS WITH KUZU

Vegan, Gluten-free, No refined sugar
SERVES 4

I like to think of this as a healthier, vegan, coconut-flavored Jell-O pudding cup. Less sweet and more sophisticated in flavor, there is something very reminiscent of the childhood dessert in texture, which I find weirdly comforting. To keep this dessert vegan, we use kuzu root, an all-natural, unprocessed thickening agent, in place of gelatin. Look for kuzu by the seaweed and agar-agar at your local health food store.

2 tablespoons kuzu root

¼ cup cold water

1 (14-ounce) can full-fat coconut milk

¼ cup coconut sugar

A pinch of salt

½ teaspoon vanilla extract

In a small saucepan, combine the kuzu and cold water and stir to dissolve. Add the coconut milk, coconut sugar, salt, and vanilla and bring to a boil over medium heat.

Let the mixture bubble, whisking continuously, until it thickens to the consistency of pudding.

Divide the pudding evenly among four ramekins, place plastic wrap directly against the surface of each pudding to prevent a film from forming, and refrigerate for at least 1 hour before serving.

COFFEE GRANITA

Vegan, Gluten-free, No refined sugar
SERVES 4

Granita is dead easy to make, but you do have to be around to scrape the ice crystals every 30 minutes, so be sure to plan ahead. This is particularly nice with a dollop of coconut whipped cream on top.

2 cups freshly brewed strong coffee or espresso, slightly cooled

3 tablespoons date syrup or maple syrup

1 teaspoon vanilla extract

Coconut Whipped Cream (page 249), for serving

Whisk together the coffee, date syrup, and vanilla, then pour into an 8 × 8-inch glass, metal, or ceramic baking dish and let cool completely. Place in a stable spot in the freezer and leave for 1 hour.

After 1 hour, use a fork to scrape the entire mixture, making sure to get the edges (this is where the granita tends to freeze first). Return to the freezer and scrape again every 30 minutes for the next 2 hours.

After 3 hours and five rounds of scraping, the granita should be ready and can be stored in the freezer as is until ready to eat.

When ready to serve, simply scrape again to loosen all the ice crystals, divide the granita and desired amount of coconut whipped cream among four glasses or bowls, and serve immediately.

FRESH PEACH MILK SHAKE

Vegan, Gluten-free, No refined sugar, Under 30 minutes
SERVES 2

Wonderfully refreshing and sweet, both of my kids scarf down these dairy-free "milk shakes" with zeal. Because peaches are the main ingredient, it's important to use really good-quality fruit. If they're out of season or you can't track down really juicy ripe ones, use 1½ cups frozen peaches instead, and add more oat milk as needed.

2 ripe peaches, pitted
1 cup non-dairy coconut ice cream

¼ cup oat or rice milk

Cut each peach into 8 pieces, then blend everything in a high-powered blender until smooth.

THE BASICS

In cooking, as in anything, it's the details that make all the difference. Here you'll find a killer granola (page 252), a bunch of easy and flavorful salsas (pages 254, 256, and 257), a basil oil (page 242) I pour on just about everything, and the easiest, quickest aioli (page 248) ever. While grocery stores are beginning to carry decent versions of a lot of these items, I really prefer to make my own when I have time. And since most of them come together in under 30 minutes (and are much cheaper than the store-bought versions), I find it's worth the extra effort.

BASIC TOMATO SAUCE

Vegan, Gluten-free
MAKES ABOUT 4 CUPS

This recipe is from my first cookbook, but I wanted to include it because I make it so often at my house. My kids love this plain with pasta, but we also use it for Pita Bread Pizzas (page 73) and Crispy Polenta (page 111).

2 tablespoons olive oil

6 garlic cloves, thinly sliced

4 large fresh basil leaves

2 (28-ounce) cans whole peeled tomatoes, with their juice

Coarse salt and freshly ground black pepper

Heat the olive oil in a large sauté pan over low heat, add the garlic, and cook for 5 minutes. Add 2 of the basil leaves and stir for a minute. Add the tomatoes and their juice and the remaining 2 basil leaves. Turn the heat to high. Bring the sauce to a boil, reduce the heat to low, season with salt and pepper, and let it bubble away for 45 minutes, stirring occasionally and crushing the tomatoes with a wooden spoon. Use immediately or let cool and refrigerate.

BASIL OIL

Vegan, Gluten-free, Under 30 minutes
MAKES ABOUT ½ CUP

Drizzle this simple basil oil over Grilled Squid, White Bean, and Fennel Salad (page 143), fresh cheese, toasted bread, or any soup to add a grassy, garlicky pop.

1 cup lightly packed fresh basil leaves, roughly chopped

½ cup olive oil

1 garlic clove, minced

Salt

In a blender or food processor, combine the basil, olive oil, and garlic and blend until smooth; add salt to taste.

BBQ SAUCE

Vegan, Gluten-free
MAKES ABOUT 2 CUPS

I use this BBQ sauce on our BBQ Chicken Skewers (page 134), but it's also great on steak, ribs, salmon, or tofu. My kids like to dip French fries into it. This makes about 2 cups and keeps well in the fridge (but always disappears quickly).

1 tablespoon olive oil

1 small white onion, diced, grated, or chopped in a food processor

3 garlic cloves, minced

Salt

¾ cup ketchup

¼ cup brown rice syrup or maple syrup

1 tablespoon Dijon mustard

1 tablespoon Worcestershire sauce

3 tablespoons apple cider vinegar

Heat the oil in a medium saucepan over medium heat. Add the onion, garlic, and a large pinch of salt and cook for 10 minutes. Add the ketchup, brown rice syrup, mustard, Worcestershire, and ¾ cup water; bring the mixture to a boil, then reduce the heat and simmer gently for 15 minutes. Add the vinegar and let the mixture cool for 5 minutes before blending with an immersion blender. If not using right away, store in the fridge for up to 1 week.

BOILED EGGS

Vegetarian, Gluten-free, Under 30 minutes

If you ask me, eggs are a magic ingredient: they're cheap, easy to prepare, and full of protein. For that reason, there are a lot of recipes involving eggs in this book, and a lot of those call for boiled eggs cooked to different degrees of doneness. Our method for hard- and soft-boiling eggs and a breakdown of which recipes call for which amount of time is on the facing page. —TB

Thea is a master of getting the center of the yolk just perfect for the recipe. I set out like a scientist with a timer to learn exactly how she does it. —GP

Bring a small saucepan of water to a boil. Add the egg, making sure it is completely submerged in water, and keep the water at a steady boil over medium-high heat for the required number of minutes (we highly recommend setting a timer) for the recipe you are making (see the facing page). When the timer goes off, remove the egg and run it under cold water or plunge it briefly into an ice bath to stop the cooking. Use immediately or let cool and store in the fridge for up to 1 week. To reheat a soft-boiled egg, place it in a saucepan of simmering water for 1 minute.

CASHEW CREAM

Vegan, Gluten-free
MAKES ABOUT 1 CUP

If you're vegan (or even if you're not), you'll love this cashew "whipped cream." A high-powered blender such as a Vitamix is essential to get the right texture.

1 cup organic raw cashews, soaked in water to cover for at least 2 hours

½ cup filtered water

1 tablespoon plus 1 teaspoon maple syrup

A pinch of salt

¼ teaspoon vanilla powder or vanilla extract

Drain the cashews, then transfer them to a high-powered blender, add the remaining ingredients, and blend until smooth, about 2 minutes.

CHEAT'S AIOLI

Vegan, Gluten-free, Under 30 minutes
MAKES ABOUT ½ CUP

I couldn't live without Vegenaise and always keep a jar of it in the fridge. For this cheat's aioli, I dress it up simply with lemon, garlic, and salt. It takes 2 minutes, tastes amazing, and has multiple uses.

½ cup **Vegenaise**

½ teaspoon very finely grated or minced **lemon zest**

1 teaspoon fresh **lemon juice**

1 small **garlic clove**, very finely grated or minced

A pinch of **salt**

Combine all the ingredients in a bowl and whisk until smooth.

CILANTRO HUMMUS

Vegan, Gluten-free, Under 30 minutes
MAKES 1½ CUPS

I am firmly of the school that "cilantro is the best herb ever," and I think it makes almost everything better, including hummus. If you are one of those people who hate cilantro (and therefore love dill, a random correlation I find is almost always true), skip this recipe or substitute parsley for the cilantro. If you don't have an immersion blender, I highly recommend investing in one—they're really affordable and make cleanup a cinch.

1 (15-ounce) can **chickpeas**, drained and rinsed

Juice of ½ large **lemon**, plus more as needed

1½ teaspoons **salt**, plus more as needed

3 tablespoons **tahini**

¼ cup **olive oil**

2 **garlic cloves**, very finely minced

½ cup roughly chopped fresh **cilantro leaves**

Combine all the ingredients in a bowl with ¼ cup water and use an immersion blender to blend until smooth (alternatively, use a food processor). Adjust with more lemon, salt, or water to taste.

COCONUT WHIPPED CREAM

Vegan, Gluten-free
MAKES ABOUT 1½ CUPS

Coconut whipped cream is all the rage in the world of vegan desserts. The texture is impressively similar to that of whipped cream, and the coconut flavor pairs extremely well with a lot of sweets. It's pretty easy to whip up, but remember that the can needs to chill in the fridge overnight to ensure that the cream and the liquid separate properly.

1 (14-ounce) can full-fat coconut milk, placed in the fridge overnight*

1 tablespoon coconut sugar

A small pinch of salt

½ teaspoon vanilla extract

Scoop the solid coconut cream off the top of the can into a medium bowl. Use a fork or potato masher to break it up until slightly softened and smooth. Add the sugar, salt, and vanilla extract and whisk by hand (or with an electric beater) until it has the texture of whipped cream, about 3 minutes.

* We learned the hard way that the brand of canned coconut milk is very important here. Some coconut milks refuse to separate no matter how long they are left in the fridge, while others can be separated and whipped right off the grocery store shelf. In our experience, both Organic Thai Kitchen and Organic Native Forest brands work well, but try out a couple of different ones and don't waste your time trying to whip coconut milk that won't separate!

FRESH COCONUT MILK

Vegan, Gluten-free, Under 30 minutes
MAKES ABOUT 1½ CUPS

Fresh coconut milk is like dairy-free half-and-half, it's so creamy; and if you can find fresh cut-up coconut, it's also really easy to make. Blend some and store in the fridge for up to 4 days (though mine never lasts more than a day).

1 cup diced fresh coconut meat (roughly ¾-inch square pieces)

1½ cups filtered water

Blitz the coconut and water in a high-powered blender until very smooth; pour through a fine-mesh strainer.

DIPPING SAUCES

Here are two versatile and really easy sauces, great for dipping anything from crudités to frozen chicken nuggets. Hey, no one's perfect, right?

HONEY MUSTARD SAUCE

Gluten-free, Under 30 minutes
MAKES ABOUT ½ CUP

¼ cup Dijon mustard

3 tablespoons honey

1 teaspoon hot mustard powder

1 tablespoon very hot water

Whisk together all the ingredients.

RANCH DIP

Vegan, Gluten-free, Under 30 minutes
MAKES ABOUT ¾ CUP

½ cup Vegenaise

2 tablespoons finely chopped fresh chives

1 small garlic clove, very finely grated or minced

1 tablespoon red wine vinegar

½ teaspoon Worcestershire sauce

1 tablespoon finely chopped fresh parsley

1 teaspoon fresh lemon juice

Salt and freshly ground black pepper

Whisk together the first 7 ingredients; season with salt and pepper to taste.

FURIKAKE

Vegan, Gluten-free, Under 30 minutes
MAKES ABOUT ¾ CUP

Furikake is a popular Japanese seasoning made from nori, salt, sugar, and sesame seeds. I love sprinkling it over rice, avocado toast, or anything that needs a little extra zip. I started experimenting with making my own this year, and I must say, the resulting recipe does not disappoint. Sprinkle this over sesame noodles, congee, popcorn, or do as Gwyneth does and eat it with your fingers as a snack. —TB

2 toasted nori sheets

2 tablespoons toasted sesame seeds

2 teaspoons coconut sugar

½ teaspoon toasted sesame oil

A pinch of salt

Use your fingers to crumble the nori into very small pieces into a bowl, then add the remaining ingredients. Store in an airtight container at room temperature for up to 3 days.

GRANOLA

Vegan, Gluten-free
MAKES ABOUT 5½ CUPS

I'm addicted to this granola. It's slightly salty, slightly sweet, wonderfully crunchy, and makes the whole house smell like Thanksgiving. Buckwheat groats, which are actually seeds, can be found in the gluten-free grain section of most Whole Foods Markets or natural food stores. —TB

2 cups gluten-free rolled oats

½ cup buckwheat groats

1 cup unsweetened shredded coconut

¼ cup hemp seeds

½ cup walnut pieces, very roughly chopped

1 teaspoon coarse sea salt

⅓ cup coconut oil, melted

½ cup maple syrup

1 teaspoon vanilla extract

¼ teaspoon ground cardamom

¼ teaspoon ground cloves

Preheat the oven to 250°F.

Combine all the ingredients in a large bowl and mix well. Transfer the mixture to a large baking sheet and bake for 1 hour.

Use a large spatula to break up the granola and return to the oven for 15 minutes.

Let cool completely before eating.

PERFECTLY COOKED GRAINS

I developed these recipes for my last cookbook, *It's All Good*, but I wanted to include them here as well, because they're so useful and versatile.

PERFECTLY COOKED QUINOA

Vegan, Gluten-free, Under 30 minutes
MAKES 3 CUPS

1 cup quinoa	**Coarse sea salt**

Rinse the quinoa thoroughly in a fine-mesh strainer (although this may sound like an unnecessary step, it really makes a huge difference in flavor, since quinoa's natural coating tastes like soap).

Place the rinsed quinoa in a pot set over high heat with 1¾ cups water and a big pinch of salt. Bring the water to a boil, lower the heat, cover the pot, and cook until all the liquid has been absorbed and the quinoa's germs look like lots of little spirals, 12 to 15 minutes. Turn off the heat, place a dry paper towel between the pot and the lid, and let the quinoa sit for at least 5 minutes before giving it a fluff with a fork.

PERFECTLY COOKED BROWN RICE

Vegan, Gluten-free
MAKES 3 CUPS

1 cup short-grain brown rice	**Coarse sea salt**

Rinse the rice thoroughly in a fine-mesh strainer until the water runs clear.

Place the rinsed rice in a pot set over high heat with 1¾ cups water and a big pinch of salt. Bring the mixture to a boil, lower the heat, cover the pot, and cook until all the liquid has been absorbed and the rice is cooked through, exactly 45 minutes. Turn the heat off, place a dry paper towel between the pot and the lid, and let the rice sit for at least 5 minutes before giving it a fluff with a fork.

ROASTED TOMATO SALSA

Vegan, Gluten-free
MAKES ABOUT 3 CUPS

Roasting the tomatoes first gives this salsa a really nice roundness and hints of smoky sweet flavor. Be sure the roasted vegetables have cooled completely before blending them with the other ingredients. You want the cilantro to retain its bright flavors.

8 plum tomatoes, cut in half

4 garlic cloves, unpeeled

1 small white onion, cut into quarters, plus ½ small white onion, roughly chopped

Olive oil

A pinch of salt, plus more as needed

3 small dried chipotle peppers

½ cup chopped fresh cilantro

Freshly ground black pepper

Preheat the oven to 450°F.

Place the tomatoes, garlic cloves, and quartered onion on a baking sheet; drizzle with olive oil and season with salt. Roast for 30 minutes.

While the veggies roast, toast the chipotles in a small dry sauté pan for about 1 minute. Transfer to a bowl and cover with boiling water to rehydrate.

When the veggies are very well browned and soft, remove from the oven and let cool to room temperature.

While the veggies cool, remove the chipotles from their water bath, tear them in half, and remove most of the seeds. Roughly chop, then add them to the bowl of a food processor along with the roasted veggies, roughly chopped onion, and cilantro.

Pulse until almost smooth, then season with salt and black pepper to taste.

FRESH SALSA

Vegan, Gluten-free, Under 30 minutes
MAKES ABOUT 2½ CUPS

Because dicing a pound of tomatoes by hand is too much to ask of anyone on a weeknight, we employ our trusty food processor to do all the work here. This salsa comes together in under 10 minutes and lasts for a couple of days in the fridge. Serve it with nachos, tacos, or our breakfast Migas (page 10).

1 pound vine-ripened tomatoes

½ cup roughly chopped white onion (about ½ medium onion)

1 jalapeño, seeded and roughly diced

½ cup fresh cilantro, roughly chopped

½ teaspoon salt

Juice of 1 lime

Cut the tomatoes into quarters and remove the juice and seeds from half of them. Combine the tomatoes, onion, jalapeño, and cilantro in a food processor and pulse until finely chopped.

Add the salt and lime juice.

TOMATILLO SALSA

Vegan, Gluten-free
MAKES ABOUT 4 CUPS

I learned to make a version of this salsa at my first paid kitchen job, and have loved tomatillos ever since. The original recipe involves slowly sweating together the onion and garlic, but this shortcut version is almost as good and much easier. If you love spicy food, add another jalapeño. If not, feel free to remove the seeds to keep the heat to a minimum. —TB

1½ pounds tomatillos (about 20), husks removed, washed well

½ medium white onion, cut into ½-inch slices

2 garlic cloves, unpeeled and smashed

1 jalapeño

Salt

1 small bunch of fresh cilantro, chopped

Preheat the oven to 400°F.

Place the tomatillos, onion, garlic, and jalapeño on an aluminum foil–lined baking sheet and roast for 20 minutes. Remove the stem from the jalapeño and the skin from the garlic cloves, and blend everything in a food processor until mostly smooth. Season with salt and let cool to room temperature.

When the salsa has cooled, add the cilantro and serve or refrigerate for up to 1 week.

ACKNOWLEDGMENTS

**FOOD STYLIST
AND PRODUCER**

Susie Theodorou
Assisted by:
Dara Sutin
Sammie Bell
Theo Theodorou

PHOTOGRAPHER

Ditte Isager
Assisted by:
Jørgen Asmussen

PROP AND SET STYLIST

Christine Rudolph
Assisted by:
Carl Hjortsøe
Catrine Håland

CLOTHING STYLIST

Elizabeth Saltzman
Assisted by:
Melissa Digilio
Grace Richmond
Malin Siljing

**ART DIRECTION
AND DESIGN**

Shubhani Sarkar
Matthew Axe

**GRAND CENTRAL
LIFE & STYLE**

Karen Murgolo
Morgan Hedden

Tareth Mitch
Tom Whatley
Claire Brown
Nicole Bond

**AND A SPECIAL
THANKS TO**

Eliza Honey
Kevin Keating
Elouisa Rivera
Terry Abbott
Ninah Moolchan
Oliver Hawthorne
Victoria Ortiz
Maria Alba

Aiayu
Andrea Brugi
Borough Kitchen
Calvin Klein Home
Chemex
Christiane Perrochon
Clifton Nurseries
Cuckmere Trug Company
Daniel Smith
Dixon
Foodgear—Kai Knives
Grace Lee
Gurli Elbaekgaard
Herdmar
Howe
Janaki Larsen
Kaufmann Mercantile
Kirstie van Noort
Kjaer Weiss

Lue Brass
Mepra
Merci
Mudd Australia
The New Craftsmen
Overlap Sewing Studio
Riess Enamelware
Rina Menardi
RMS
Rush Matters/Felicity Irons
Society Linen
Stanley & Sons
Staub
Stelton/Rig-Tig
Variopinte
Vitamix
The Wooden Palate
Zani Zani
Zwilling

Artichoke Hampstead
  +44 20 7431 4630
E. Dehilerin
  +33 1 42 36 53 13
La Fromagerie
  +44 20 7935 0341
G. Detou
  +33 1 42 36 54 67
Izraël
  +33 1 42 72 66 23

INDEX